To
Betty Berg Leonard

Send your good men into the ministry, but send your best into politics. Because in the ministry, it all depends on the Spirit, but in politics you have shades of gray, ambiguities, and you need the finest people.

—Martin Luther

Freeman

the governor years

1955–1960

Rodney E. Leonard

Hubert H. Humphrey Institute of Public Affairs

Minneapolis

2003

On the Cover
Gov. Orville L. Freeman waves to delegates at the 1960 Democratic
National Convention in Los Angeles after nominating
Sen. John F. Kennedy for president.

Photo Sources
Front cover, frontispiece, and pp. 6, 36, 64, and 222, courtesy of Jane Freeman;
pp. 16 and 114, Minnesota Historical Society; p. 88 © *Bettmann/CORBIS,*
used by permission; pp. 144 and back cover, Hubert H. Humphrey Institute
of Public Affairs; pp. 178 and 194, University of Minnesota Alumni Associa-
tion (*Minnesota* magazine).

Editing, Design, Production
E. B. Green Editorial, St. Paul, Minnesota

Indexing
Patricia Green, Homer, Alaska

Printing
Sexton Printing, Inc., St. Paul, Minnesota

Binding
Muscle Bound Bindery, Minneapolis

———————

Contents

Preface

F resh from the Korean War, I enrolled as a graduate student in the University of Minnesota School of Journalism in the fall of 1953. Four years later, in the spring of 1957, I was—much to the dismay of my Republican in-laws—official press secretary in the office of Gov. Orville L. Freeman of Minnesota. I had read about Steve Early, press secretary to President Harry S. Truman, and that was as much of the job as I knew.

Only three other staff assistants worked in the office. Dorothy Jacobson was an academician who wrote speeches and smoked cigarettes incessantly. Freeman's executive secretary, Tom Hughes, hired me, didn't smoke, and drank only beer. Cy Magnuson, a gentle soul who neither smoke nor drank and didn't talk much, handled citizen inquiries and complaints. Five others also worked there. Billy Williams, a kindly man regarded as a living institution, had been special aide to every governor since before I was born. A lone receptionist, Barbara Lynch, fielded every call and patiently answered the questions of the stream of visitors wandering in and out of the office. A three-person secretarial staff, led by Governor Freeman's personal secretary, worked in a back office.

No one knew what a press secretary was supposed to do, and no one asked me. But everyone welcomed me, and so I began. A blizzard of memos, copies of reports with Freeman's cryptic comments and questions, studies, letters from people he had met, requests for information, directions for press releases, and requests for speech drafts soon engulfed my desk. They never stopped coming.

I quickly learned I was the staff expert on consumer policy and sometimes on tax policy, conservation, veterans' affairs, and other issues. I learned that we could rarely make decisions with as much knowledge as we wished and that failing to decide could be the worst decision of all. I briefed reporters, prepared press releases, wrote speeches, summarized reports, and conspired with Dorothy and Tom to get Freeman to state what he sometimes was reluctant to say—or to refrain from characterizing in public his private thoughts about an opponent's antecedents. It was a wonderful time. I marveled then as now at my good fortune in parachuting into a drama in which all the other players had devoted more than a decade to electing the first DFL governor.

Nowhere else is there an assessment of Freeman's contribution as the first Minnesotan of the Democratic-Farmer-Labor Party (DFL) to be elected governor. And so this study of Orville L. Freeman's three gubernatorial terms—from 1955 to 1960—means to fill that gap.

The Minnesota History Center is a rich depository of information from the period, particularly contained in the copious personal files of Jane and Orville Freeman and his associates in the governor's office, in the official files of the Office of the Governor, oral histories of legislators, interviews conducted for other historical projects, and the avalanche of news items contained in the microfilms of Minnesota newspapers. In addition, I have been able to interview many of the individuals who participated in the events shaping Minnesota governance at the time. What emerges is a fascinating panorama of the journey of Minnesota from a somewhat conservative state of complacency to an active commitment to liberalism. During the six years Freeman served as governor, a majority of Minnesotans came to support the vision of a first-class education system, of conservation and environmental protection, health and social services, and of community and business development, all while insisting on ethical government to ensure public trust. Freeman did not originate this consensus, but he distilled it as a political vision planted in the DFL. This book describes how he communicated the message, organized the party as an instrument to gain the political power essential to authorizing liberal programs, and developed a strategy to fund them.

Many friends and co-conspirators assisted in this effor. I thank Jane Shields Freeman for her unfailing support and patience and for the time she has given to filling in the blanks, adding insights and gently correcting my errors. Mike and Connie Freeman gave great help and support and reviewed the manuscript. Judge Gerald Heaney, Don and Arvonne Fraser, Arthur Naftalin, Leonard Lindquist, Lee Loevenger, and many others shared their recollections of the times and events. Jane Leonard and Lori Lippert, John Leonard, Cia Guidice, and Karl and Karin Sonneman read, commented on, and made suggestions on the manuscript. I am grateful to the staff of the Minnesota Historical Society for assisting in my research. Steve Sandell of the Humphrey Institute Forum lent especially helpful support during my research and writing. Ellen Green contributed to clarity of thought and ease of reading as final editor of the manuscript.

And I'm especially thankful to Betty Berg Leonard for her support, her patience, and her early warnings not to write the manuscript like a speech. I regret I cannot give her the first copy of the publication and say that I took her advice, but she knows that already.

—Rod Leonard

Introduction

Minnesota voters chose Orville L. Freeman as governor in 1954, ending a 17-year Republican lock on state government. Freeman was 36 years old, the second youngest governor in Minnesota's history. He had been actively involved in the political campaigns of the Democratic-Farmer-Labor Party (DFL) since returning from military service in 1944. He was a U.S. Marine lieutenant whose combat experience ended abruptly in 1943 on Bougainville Island in the South Pacific, when a Japanese machine-gun bullet tore away much of his lower left jaw. A decade later he was the first DFL governor.

This work examines six events and issues defining Freeman's stewardship during three terms as governor of Minnesota, from 1954 to 1960. During that period the DFL emerged as well, uniquely blending organizational discipline with social issues to shape public debate on governance during the second half of the 20th century. This achievement was largely the result of Freeman's vision.

As an executive, Freeman considered politics integral to the function of governance. He understood that government could not respond to the wishes of the governed without the institutions of government. Neither could public institutions function without the political party, a nongovernment institution capable of identifying and translating social and economic priorities into policy. His goal was to build institutions, both public and private, that would strengthen the process of governance. Thus Freeman viewed his responsibility as governor to act not only as the chief executive of Minnesota but also as the leader of the DFL. From that perspective, these studies comprise an analysis of Minnesota consensus on the postwar direction of the state developing in parallel with the emergence of the DFL from the chrysalis of its first decade.

This work inevitably touches on the relationship between Orville Freeman and his lifelong friend and political partner Hubert H. Humphrey. While both were intimately involved in the formation of the DFL, Freeman was the midwife of its postwar creation as the dominant party in the state. Humphrey, Freeman's partner in politics and mutually affectionate friend, had won the 1948 election for the U.S. Senate. Freeman was his campaign manager. Their friendship withstood all the temptations and strain endemic to politics because no misunderstanding was possible. Freeman knew Humphrey was totally ruthless as a candidate. His own personal disappointment might be a consequence of this trait, but Freeman knew that loyalty was key to their bond. And that bond was key to the organizational success of the DFL—that is, winning elections. At the same time Humphrey knew that Freeman based his political commitments on deeply held principles and that he could reliably anticipate Freeman's behavior under pressure. With no disagreement on policy goals, their relationship was the bond holding together the ascent of the DFL.

The dreams and hopes of a majority of Minnesotans for their state shifted with Freeman's election, and the DFL became a different kind of political party after 1954. The party enlarged the nexus between a fear of change and an impatience with the status quo, ensuring the political space for economic opportunity and social justice to grow.

In his political dreams, his mother recalled, Freeman wanted to be governor. Humphrey wanted to go to Washington as a senator. In achieving those dreams, the Romulus and Remus of Minnesota's DFL laid bare their underlying political differences. Humphrey won election in 1948—a political victory that Freeman organized but that was largely Humphrey's personal achievement. The DFL played only a marginal, symbolic role. Six years later Humphrey won reelection while Freeman and the DFL ticket swept Republican incumbents out of state government in a campaign organized around a new DFL. The 1954 campaign proved again that Humphrey was a magnetic political personality. The 1956 election demonstrated that Freeman was leader of the DFL, an institution riding above the surge of Pres. Dwight D. Eisenhower's reelection. It was an organization able to provide vision for an enduring majority of Minnesotans.

Orville L. Freeman was born May 9, 1918, and grew up in south Minneapolis. His father, a merchant, provided well enough for the family, but Freeman and his brother had to work for their education beyond high school. Active in athletics at South Minneapolis High, Freeman also gained an early reputation as a student. He enjoyed play, but his pals knew the books came first. Still, his ability in football was his ticket in 1938 to the University of Minnesota. Freeman earned the backup quarterback role on Bernie Bierman's Golden Gopher football team while scrubbing walls for 35 cents an hour at University Hospital. Study didn't interfere with his extracurricular activities, nor did academics suffer. Freeman was an honors student, and Coach Bierman praised him as much for raising the grade-point average of the football squad as for the depth he brought to the quarterback position.

Freeman gravitated to the political-science orbit of a group of students and instructors including Humphrey, who endlessly discussed politics. Humphrey, a graduate student, invited Freeman to debate, and the duo became the university's championship debate team. Freeman won election as president of the student body as an undergraduate. Jane Shields, a recent undergraduate arrival from North Carolina, joined him in student government and was elected secretary. They fell in love, and announced their engagement to Eleanor Roosevelt in a student-union elevator while escorting the observant and bemused First Lady to campus events. Orville and Jane married May 2, 1942, shortly before Orville went to the South Pacific as a newly commissioned U.S. Marine lieutenant. Following extensive rehabilitation for a combat injury on Bougainville Island, he returned to Minneapolis in 1944 and was graduated from the University of Minnesota Law School in 1946. Then he joined the new firm of Larson, Loevinger, Lindquist and Freeman, committed to supporting the participation in public service of its partners. Thus Freeman was able to dedicate the next eight years to creating the DFL.

The six events and issues treated here are among many that demonstrate Freeman's governorship. Each shows how his personal character, energy, determination, intelligence, and commitment met the test of the crucible of governance, in a process enabling the DFL to mature as an institution and enhancing the capacity of state government during the explosive period of growth in Minnesota:

1. The 1954 election: Freeman transformed an effort largely staffed by volunteers, and first conceived as a defensive strategy to ensure the reelection of Humphrey, into a winning campaign. His innovations in communications and organizational methods became the hallmark of modern political campaigns.

2. The 1956 campaign: Armed with the record of a contentious but fruitful 1955 legislative session, Freeman faced a crucial re-election test against a popular Republican opponent expecting the coattails of President Eisenhower to provide the margin of victory. Demonstrating that the public could trust the DFL to govern effectively, Freeman further refined campaign techniques in his dual role as governor and head of the DFL.

3. The 1958 campaign: With two successful legislative sessions plus innovative tax-reform proposals, government reorganization, education, welfare, and other programs under his belt, Freeman led a 1958 campaign for reelection that brought Minnesota its second national DFL senator. New methods and practices in planning, fundraising, coordination of candidates, and execution resulted in a campaign organization considered the best ever assembled in postwar Minnesota politics.

4. Albert Lea and the strike at Wilson and Company: Unexpected events tested the mettle of political leaders and political parties. Freeman averted violence by closing the Wilson meatpacking plant in Albert Lea when packinghouse workers struck against the management's rejection of collective bargaining. The restoration of community peace resulted in resolution of the dispute through collective bargaining of union and management.

5. Withholding and tax reform: Confrontation over tax policy became the epic political conflict of the 1950s, as Freeman and the DFL sought to modernize the tax structure into a stable framework to pay for government and public services. The issue was the withholding of state income-tax payments, a centerpiece of the DFL tax-reform program.

6. Policies and programs: As leader of the DFL, Freeman proposed and advanced a full range of programs for state services. He campaigned ceaselessly for DFL programs, making endless rounds of speeches to groups and organizations, writing legislative messages, holding press conferences and media interviews. Freeman's small staff transformed information from state agencies and departments into educational material intended as much for use by DFLers to explain the mission of government as for informing the general public of its work.

*Vice President of the United States Hubert H. Humphrey, left, and
Secretary of Agriculture Orville L. Freeman, right, in 1965*

—1—

Prologue

Not until ten years after its birth in 1944 was the Democratic-Farmer-Labor Party able to assert a commanding statewide political presence. Even at the start of 1954, that future was hard to predict.

Harold Stassen had ended the Republicans' political drought of the 1930s by defeating the last Farmer-Labor governor, Elmer Benson, in 1938. The GOP gained a controlling majority in the Minnesota Senate and House of Representatives by 1940, under the nonpartisan but appropriate label of the Conservative caucus. Republican dominance of state politics had since been unshakable.

Hubert H. Humphrey's election to the U.S. Senate in 1948 had retired Joseph Hurst Ball, a tired Republican elected in the midst of World War II. But the most the DFL otherwise had achieved in any two-year election cycle was to send three persons to Congress, one each from the city of St. Paul, the Iron Range, and the farming counties of northwestern Minnesota. The latter was a region of thin soil as unforgiving to farmers as they were of Ezra Taft Benson, then President Dwight D. Eisenhower's secretary of agriculture. These liberal

Minnesota strongholds predictably elected DFL candidates to Congress regardless of the statewide political fortunes of the Republicans.

So, with Senator Humphrey facing reelection, the DFL was on the outside looking in. Any political analyst would have considered him vulnerable. His election in 1948 had been no great victory as opponent Ball was not an effective campaigner. Even in the 1942 Senate race Ball had not received a majority—the vote had split three ways in his defeat of the Farmer-Labor and Democratic opponents. Humphrey's opposition in 1954 likely would be Val Bjornson, a popular Republican moderate currently serving as state treasurer. The DFL, rebuffed in three campaigns, held no elected state office, and it had lost every race for congressional seats outside the liberal redoubts. There was little to bolster hope for the DFL as an effective (winning) party statewide.

Humphrey had other reasons for concern. His first term in the Senate was a disaster. His stirring oratory at the 1948 national Democratic convention gave him nationwide exposure while leading to an ignominious defeat of Southern party leaders over the civil-rights plank of its platform. Retribution awaited. Southern senators rejected his proffered friendship, reducing Humphrey to tears on his daily drive home from work.[1] He contributed to the isolation by breaking every rule of comity in the Senate, first an exclusive club and then an institution of democratic governance. Even his admirers complained that he couldn't shut up. The response to his 1949 resolution to abolish a committee chaired by Sen. Harry Byrd of Virginia was a four-hour cascade of venom from the senators of every state of the South, a personal assault unrivaled before or since. He was assigned to the least important Senate committees and became the butt of Vice President Alben W. Barkley's personal jokes.[2]

Humphrey was not a happy camper.[3] Only his reelection could vindicate his status as an equal member of the U.S. Senate. More compelling was his fear that the chances for his lifelong dream of becoming president, a passion driving all his political actions, would end abruptly. He and Sen. Lyndon B. Johnson of Texas, acknowledging their mutual vision of the presidential office as the Holy Grail, had begun an intricate political dance, warily circling in search for advantage and power.[4] If Humphrey was to continue the dance, he first had to win reelection.

Humphrey turned to an old and trusted friend. Orville L. Freeman was the architect of the DFL as an activist party with a strong postwar anti-Communist bias. He had managed Humphrey's senatorial campaign in 1948 but did not accompany Humphrey to Washington as chief of the new senator's staff.[5] Freeman had decided to stay in Minnesota to concentrate on building the DFL as an effective statewide political force—and to run for governor.[6] He had become a partner in Larson, Loevinger, Lindquist and Freeman, a law firm organized with the explicit belief that its members must be able to devote significant time to public service. Recognizing he could trust his friend to protect the home base, Humphrey wisely did not make an issue of Freeman joining him in Washington.[7]

Freeman had experienced success first in leading a reform-group takeover of the DFL from Farmer-Labor activists and then in managing the Humphrey campaign. These achievements earned him the post of state DFL chair in 1948. Two years later, the party nominated its acknowledged leader for attorney general, but Freeman lost—badly. Karl F. Rolvaag, a tank officer in Europe during World War II and later governor of Minnesota, replaced Freeman as DFL chair in 1952. Freeman ran that year as the DFL candidate for governor and lost again. Republican C. Elmer Anderson, who had served six terms (also 1939–1943) as lieutenant governor, won the governor's race that year.[8]

Republican candidates everywhere attained success in 1952 on the coattails of Dwight "I Like Ike" Eisenhower, the GOP presidential candidate. Freeman, however, with little reason other than his own conviction, had believed *he* could win in Minnesota, and his loss to Anderson was personally devastating. Almost 35, Freeman had spent ten years preparing for success yet apparently had failed as a political leader. Politics was his passion, thanks to the support of his law firm, but now he faced the reality of life as the family breadwinner. He and Jane Freeman were responsible for two children. They had little money, and he saw it as his duty to begin the full-time practice of law to build a secure future for his family.

Accordingly, Freeman told Humphrey in January 1953 of his plan to close the DFL state office, which he had personally financed. He offered to continue its operation until Humphrey could decide what he wanted to do. Freeman said the rent was minimal; he would leave the few pieces of furniture and equipment.[9]

Freeman, a fearlessly outspoken, take-charge personality with an in-your-face political style, momentarily and uncharacteristically had lost his confidence. He was not alone. The young DFL leaders, all of whom had studied but not experienced the prewar political struggles in Minnesota, reached consensus in the face of political crisis. Examining the prospects for Humphrey's 1954 reelection from the perspective of a decade of DFL losses, they decided to focus all their energy and resources on his campaign.

Vice President Richard Nixon had targeted Senator Humphrey, a thorn under President Eisenhower's saddle as well as in the side of Senate leadership, for political extinction. The DFL leaders could not confidently assess this as a political factor, but none could ignore it. Freeman's frustration with and Humphrey's low level of confidence in the DFL organization were understandable. But as events demonstrated, the bird-in-the-hand-is-worth-two-in-the-bush strategy seriously mispredicted the evolving political fortunes of the DFL.

Viewed from another perspective, the DFL had run a competitive race in 1952. The vote for the candidate for governor generally determines the fate of candidates for other state elective offices. A five-point swing in 1952, for example, when the Eisenhower landslide swept Republicans into office everywhere, would have elected Freeman and the DFL ticket. The Freeman percentage of votes cast for governor, other than for the 1948 election, was the best showing in ten years by any DFL candidate for governor.

Over the previous 32 years in 16 two-year election cycles, a 5 percent swing in the vote would have changed the outcome in nine gubernatorial elections. Then as now, the core vote of Republicans and Democrats was not sufficient to win Minnesota elections consistently. The swing voter generally has controlled Minnesota elections in the 20th century except for two periods. Floyd B. Olson led the Farmer-Labor Party to a stunning sequence of four victories starting in 1930 as the Great Depression first demolished the farm economy and then destroyed urban jobs. The Farmer-Labor Party's bedrock support became evident in the 1932 election, when he won more than 72 of every 100 votes cast, leaving the GOP with only 28. In the four campaigns from 1930 to 1936, the Farmer-Laborites gained more then six of ten voters in the governor's race, with Elmer Benson winning 61 to 39 percent in 1936.[10]

Republicans returned the favor, sweeping the gubernatorial campaign from 1938 through 1952 to win three of the eight elections by margins greater than 60 percent. Harold Stassen ousted Elmer Benson for governor in 1938 by 61 to 39 percent, though a 5 percent shift in the two subsequent elections won by Stassen would have given those races to the Farmer-Laborites. Then Republican Luther W. Youngdahl nailed down the governor's office in three campaigns—1946, 1948, and 1950. Because his emphasis on mental-health reforms gave the Republicans a moderately liberal tinge, the DFL was competitive in only one of those races.

Swing voters, by definition, were more liberal than bedrock Republicans with a laissez-faire outlook and less so than diehard DFL supporters, particularly those from the Farmer-Labor wing on the far left. But the economic, social, and cultural profile of the American voter, especially the swing voter, was changing. A shift in voting patterns, evolving from the influx of voters assembled from two huge cultural blocs after World War II, changed postwar politics across the nation as well as in Minnesota. Veterans like Freeman, Gerald W. Heaney, and Karl Rolvaag returned from the war determined to succeed. If the United States could win World War II, then its government could help individuals achieve personal, family, and economic goals.

And they expected help from the government in rebuilding their lives. The veterans, intent on graduating with degrees as quickly as possible, overwhelmed Minnesota colleges and universities. They raised the grade curve, giving high-school freshmen a new perspective on academic competition. Many veterans had families, wanted jobs, homes, health services, roads, and schools for children. If government could organize resources to end the Great Depression and win a world war, returning veterans had reason to believe that government could make the dreams of a peaceful world come true.

Pragmatically, veterans were willing to take a chance—the thought of an activist government did not trouble them nearly as much as it did the GOP. The war had been a liberating experience. They had left home freshly graduated from high school or as accountants, teachers, welders, plumbers, and ditch diggers and returned wearing sergeants' stripes and captains' bars. They were confident they could set federal policies to provide the resources for building new communities. The GI Bill for college scholarships was a down payment on a future full of promise.

The other newly liberated group with a political agenda was that of women voters, who had achieved suffrage in 1919. Ten years later, hardly time to catch a breath in politics, the Great Depression began, then continued until its full resolution by World War II. These calamitous events focused political energy first on economic recovery and then on military victory. Now, some 30 years after winning the right to vote, women could to return to organizing, working to shape and guide public policy on issues important to them. Holding the same goals identified by veterans, they also wanted to transform social values into public policy, especially equality and an end to discrimination. They wanted equal pay for equal work and an end to deep-seated gender prejudice in schools, sports, the workplace, law, medicine, and politics. They wanted the right to own property. And they could achieve the changes they wanted only through public policy and the passage of new laws. Government was a friend promising help.

These forces were shifting the political equations in many if not most states. In Massachusetts, for example, the voters elected Democratic Gov. Paul A. Dever, sweeping 27 Republicans from its General Court (the equivalent of Minnesota's House of Representatives) to give Democrats a one-vote margin in 1948. Tip O'Neill, house minority leader in 1947, had directed the legislative campaign ending decades of GOP control, and the General Court elected him speaker. Working with a single-vote margin, O'Neill passed 810 bills sent by Dever to raise taxes and provide funds to build the Massachusetts Turnpike, enlarge mental-health-care services, stave off a Boston subway-fare increase, raise minimum wages, and provide financial aid for veterans. Eerily anticipating the shift in Minnesota's future in 1954, the players in Massachusetts drew the political lines for future postwar legislative confrontations in other state governments. The *Boston Herald* could only sputter that the legislature "squandered funds recklessly, created needless jobs, and was utterly without conscience."

That the controlling middle of the state's voting public perhaps was shifting toward DFL issues held scant promise for the nervous Humphrey and a DFL leadership with skills yet unconfirmed. What had happened in Massachusetts a decade earlier, where politics was a brass-knuckles affair, seemed to hold little relevance for Minnesota.[11]

Notwithstanding Nixon's attacks on Humphrey, the DFL had little choice other than to support him, a situation that worked perversely to its advantage. Contrary to Humphrey's lack of confidence in the DFL organization, the party had active members throughout the state.[12] The problem for its leadership was a tendency towards an indifference to discipline laced with fractious internal combat. The "DFL ticket" was a misnomer. No DFL convention endorsed its candidates; rather they ran in an open primary. DFL designation was all they shared. They raised their own individual funds, shared no advertising and promotion, paid little or no attention to each other or to party officials, and rarely appeared together at political rallies. Instead of knocking heads publicly to achieve discipline in support of the DFL platform and convention-endorsed candidates, Senator Humphrey chose to ignore the issue and ride above the fray.[13]

The DFL leadership, particularly its central (executive) committee, exploited the convergence around Humphrey to emphasize party discipline.[14] This was necessary both to his reelection and as a statement of the party's commitment to accountability. The DFL platform called for party designation of state legislators, arguing that voters must hold the parties accountable for legislative programs and actions.

Humphrey and his advisors wanted a state ticket with the least political drag on the senator's reelection campaign.[15] The candidate for governor must cause Humphrey the least political harm. Freeman did not argue with the conventional wisdom. He believed he was the best choice but that he would not win a rematch with Anderson.[16] Mindful of the whisperings that he was damaged goods, he had decided to retire from an active role in DFL politics. He would accept the nomination, he told Humphrey and the DFL leadership, but he would not campaign for endorsement. As a result, Humphrey, his staff, and the DFL central committee were united in rebuffing trial balloons launched by Twin Cities and Greater Minnesota activists seeking the DFL endorsement for governor.

Freeman's reluctant posturing became continuing news as the date for the state DFL convention in Albert Lea drew near. Reporters hinted broadly that he would gain the endorsement. His rivals for nomination could always get news coverage by railing at unnamed "party bosses" said to control the convention.[17] The second ballot on the final day of the convention gave Freeman the nomination. The delegates had selected a DFL candidate! More significantly, the DFL had chosen the campaign director for its ticket—the party would win overwhelmingly and greatly build its confidence.

As gubernatorial nominee and head of the DFL, Freeman's goal was to build a political party capable of governance. To succeed, he had to accomplish five objectives:

1. The DFL must achieve status enough to function as a coordinating mechanism for consensus.
2. The DFL must achieve consensus among economic, social, and cultural interests capable of reaching a critical political mass—a majority of at least one vote in the statehouse.
3. The DFL must create momentum in political (government), social, intellectual, economic, and organizational arenas.
4. The DFL must gain the educational capacity to inform key audiences—academics, the public, government institutions, the press, and party activists.
5. The DFL must isolate political opponents within a nonpartisan context while keeping political and policy goals at the fore.

Freeman's first task was to build the political mass critical to winning the 1954 election.

Orville L. Freeman (center, on ladder) worked with other DFLers to clean up the party's donated campaign headquarters in summer 1954.

—2—

The 1954 Campaign

O rville L. Freeman left Albert Lea on Sunday, April 6, 1954, as the DFL-endorsed candidate for governor. He had not campaigned for the privilege. Neither did he believe he could win the rematch with his 1952 opponent, Gov. C. Elmer Anderson. He had agreed to run at the pleading of Sen. Hubert H. Humphrey and other leaders of the DFL. All were friends with whom he had shared a decade of frustration in trying to build a viable alternative to the Republican Party in Minnesota. They commonly believed the GOP failed to provide the leadership necessary to tap the economic, social, and educational potential essential to future progress in the state. They also believed Freeman probably could not win the election. But they shared his and Senator Humphrey's view that any other DFL gubernatorial candidate would campaign poorly and thus threaten the senator's prospects for reelection.

Returning home to Minneapolis on U.S. Highway 52, Freeman stopped in Northfield and there experienced an epiphany. As he explained in a letter to Humphrey: "Last night I spoke to the Young DFL at Carleton College . . . Where two years ago a dozen people

17

turned out, there were at least 300 last night, with a most enthusiastic response, including a standing ovation, which I never earned before."[1] The Carleton experience was also a premonition. Freeman's letter rejected the prevailing view of DFL leaders that he could not defeat Governor Anderson. It represented a new beginning in his relationship with Humphrey. "I sense a new feeling where I am concerned in most quarters, and it really helps my mental and emotional attitude a great deal. I really believe I can win this time."

Others in the DFL shared Freeman's newfound optimism. William (Bill) Kubicek, for one, had grown increasingly impatient since the 1952 election. He believed Freeman *could* be elected in 1954. A faculty member at the University of Minnesota Medical School, Dr. Kubicek had been active in DFL campaigns since 1944. He had been elected to the DFL executive committee with Dorothy Jacobson, Gerald Heaney, Eugenie Anderson, and others members of the reform group that took control of the DFL in 1948.

Kubicek had managed Freeman's campaigns for attorney general in 1950 and governor in 1952, losing both times. The losses were hard to swallow, but the DFL was beginning to come within striking distance. State government, especially the prize of the governor's office, defines a political party's effectiveness and determines its public status. The real test of the party, Kubicek knew, was to wrest from the GOP the control of state government it had held since 1938. Freeman and other DFL leaders had worked ceaselessly to build a network of DFL partisans across Minnesota. Nevertheless, most voters seemed unaware of or indifferent to campaign tactics essentially unchanged since Minnesota became a state. Candidates traversed the state to create visibility but relied on political supporters in local communities and counties to build a constituency emerging only as voters cast their ballots. Traditional campaigning consumed enormous time and resources but reached only a small percentage of voters. Kubicek wanted instead to convince a majority of voters to define their individual and community interests in relation to a political party in control of government. He wanted them to identify with the DFL.

Freeman drove hard, trying to change the political inertia. While campaigning in 1950 along border counties of southern Minnesota, for example, Freeman wandered farther south than he realized. In one town he introduced himself as a candidate for attorney general.

"Attorney general of what?" a man asked.

"Minnesota, of course," Freeman replied.

"This is Iowa," the man said, pointing north, "Minnesota's there."[2]

No matter how hard and long Freeman worked, he could not connect personally with enough voters to overcome the political inertia that had given the GOP control in the state. Both Freeman and Kubicek realized they needed new techniques to break out of the DFL campaign mold. Kubicek had an idea that might work.[3] Both an electrical engineer and a professor of physical medicine, Kubicek made politics his passion. Among the technologies studied in 1953 for possible medical application was that of television. As Kubicek reviewed the potential of the medium for conveying information between and among doctors, researchers, hospital staffs, and patients, he made a serendipitous leap, merging vocation and avocation in a new technique for campaigning.

Anticipating television's potential to communicate ideas, form perceptions, and bridge geographical isolation, Kubicek envisioned a single broadcast preempting all other programming. He would buy the same time period on all television stations to telecast the same program statewide. Regardless of the station, a single message would reach all Minnesota voters at the same time. When he broached the idea to other DFL leaders, the immediate reaction was mostly negative. Voters would resent the program, they said. "You force people to listen to this by taking every television station in the state, and you're going to create a lot of ill will."[4] TV stations wouldn't agree to the idea, others said.[5] Kubicek was undeterred. The unique nature of such a broadcast apparently intrigued Minnesotans when they viewed it in 1954. Neither the participating stations nor the DFL received many complaints, Kubicek recalled.[6]

The live telecast ran on election eve for a half-hour. DFL candidates for 17 state and national offices participated, Humphrey and Freeman each with five-minute segments.[7] The two alternated in making ten-second introductions of the other candidates on the ticket, each of whom had a one-minute spot. Two cameras, alternately used, ensured that each candidate spoke no longer than 60 seconds. Most of the candidates had never before appeared on television, and even those who had worked before a TV camera were unfamiliar with the idea of devoting a one-minute appearance to one idea or issue. By alternating the cameras, the director could cut the microphone on a speaker after one minute and shift to the next candidate. Meanwhile a third camera focused on Freeman's or Humphrey's next introduction.[8]

The telecast reached an estimated audience of nearly a million viewers, succeeding in its principal objective.[9] Minnesota voters could see all the DFL candidates together as real people, some good speakers and some not, all running on one ticket, all asking for support on election day. Because the initial statewide telecast ran live, it left no room for errors or editing. Organizing a live program providing 17 people a live platform from which to speak on political issues—without falling into chaos—was no small feat. The statewide telecast not only made TV history but also conveyed that the DFL was a party of innovation accountable to voters.

Frustration over traditional campaign practices led Kubicek to develop another technique in 1954, adding to the perception of the DFL as a party of innovation. Candidates, then as now, routinely walked neighborhoods door to door, leaving political flyers touting their virtues at each home. Every candidate for county or city office and for seats in the Minnesota House and Senate spent hours this way, as did armies of volunteer supporters. Walking neighborhoods is a vital political technique, but it consumes enormous amounts of time better spent elsewhere, especially by candidates for statewide office. The challenge for Kubicek was to reach every household with a flyer, at minimal cost in time and money, that would convey the perception that all DFL candidates were running on the same ticket.

The solution was the sample ballot, then a startling innovation. Kubicek developed it with the help of Gerry Dillon, a Minneapolis printing company executive. Dillon had experimented with blanket mailings of sales promotions to households in limited geographical areas, such as urban and suburban census tracts. Kubicek recognized that employing the focused mailing method pioneered commercially by Dillon would enable the DFL to reach nearly all the voters in specific legislative districts. The sample ballot conveyed to voters that the party ticket reached from Humphrey and Freeman at the top, to congressional and state legislative candidates, and beyond.

The idea appealed to DFL candidates for seats in the U.S. House of Representatives, most of whom were contemporaries of Freeman (36 years old), and Humphrey (37 when first elected to the U.S. Senate). Many House candidates were running for office for the first time. The mail ballot enabled them to reach every household in their districts with at least one piece of campaign literature and to show they were part of the DFL ticket.[10]

The statewide telecast of the DFL ticket, together with a neighborhood sample ballot repeating information about the ticket, combined in 1954 to link the party to significant new demographic trends in the state. Television changed the way people viewed the world and, with the printed sample ballot, introduced the DFL to the suburbs. These new communities were changing how people related to each other and thought about themselves.

Party Discipline

Trust is difficult in any relationship, but nothing is more essential in politics. For the Minnesota voter in 1954, the world was in flux. World War II had ended, leaving a physically unscarred nation, the most powerful economic and military force in the world. Democratic, global leadership was vital, but millions of returning veterans were more concerned with building families and new lives. While the national government was spending billions of dollars to rebuild war-torn Europe and strengthen the American military after the Korean War, there had been little investment in infrastructures supporting public services.

The focus at the Minnesota State Capitol was on homes, jobs, earning an income, schools, neighborhoods, and communities. The baby boom had begun, and schools were overcrowded. New neighborhoods sprang up overnight in cities and suburbs, but services were poor and roads inadequate. Transportation to work, stores and shops, schools, and recreation spots was lacking. The pace of change in farming, accelerated by postwar demand for food in Europe and Japan at an unsustainable level, forced an increasing number of families off the farm and into urban areas unprepared for the influx. Communities once enjoying a comfortable, rhythmic, social, cultural, and economic existence related to farming now had to redefine their futures. The burden would overwhelm local democracy.

In winning World War II the American people learned a useful lesson—that its government could organize its resources to achieve common goals. Prewar political issues were largely irrelevant to voters reevaluating the role of government in their lives in 1954. In the process, citizens must decide which political party to trust with the task of leadership. The DFL and the GOP both had deep roots in Minnesota. Which party gained control of state government would depend on voters caught between the fear of change and a frustration with the status quo. In the 1930s, as the recession deepened, voters had put their trust in Floyd B. Olson and the Farmer-Labor Party. With the apparent waning of the Great Depression, Farmer-Laborism seemed too radical, and the voters chose Harold Stassen and the Republicans.

These events were history, viewed romantically by some and with indifference by others as the 1954 election approached. The campaign led to a decisive shift in voter sentiment when Minnesotans chose the DFL as the party to trust. And the DFL dominated politics in the state for the next 45 years.

Events large and small built the credibility of the DFL, giving the bond of public trust its strength. One struggle led by Freeman in 1948, over control of the DFL, ended perceptions of party radicalism.[11] Now voters perceived the DFL as an innovative force, especially in its employment of campaign techniques brought by Kubicek to the 1954 campaign. Breaking with nonpartisan tradition, the DFL asked voters to hold the party accountable for its ideas by identifying legislative candidates according to party affiliation.

Party discipline also gave the DFL the cohesion essential to a political party committed to issues and ideas, a less publicly dramatic approach than politics by personality. Party discipline contributed to and was reinforced by electoral successes and legislative achievements after the 1954 election. A dramatic event, now mostly forgotten, illustrates the evolution of discipline as a positive force within the DFL.

Koscie Marsh of St. Paul had gained endorsement for his candidacy for secretary of state, a glorified keeper of records, at the 1954 state DFL convention in Albert Lea. The party platform included a resolution opposing legalized gambling. Nonetheless, while campaigning in June, Marsh endorsed pari-mutuel betting in Minnesota. The DFL executive committee recoiled in astonishment, horrified that the DFL might be tagged with legalized gambling. Furthermore, it was upset that he had unleashed the idea without warning, angry that he had introduced policy issues contrary to the platform "in conflict with the principles of the party."[12]

Swift action was necessary. The DFL executive committee quickly convened, then argued for several hours. Marsh attended the meeting, saying Minnesota voters should decide the issue. The committee could issue a statement rejecting the lottery proposal, one participant suggested. "Absolutely not," said Dorothy Jacobson, assistant professor of government at Macalester College in St. Paul.[13] She offered a motion to remove Marsh as the endorsed candidate for secretary of state, which the committee approved.

Under party rules, however, only the state convention could vote to remove an endorsed candidate. Organizing a meeting of the convention would take weeks and require funds the DFL could ill afford. Jacobson proposed sending a mail ballot to the chairs of DFL committees in county and district organizations. But a quick reading of the DFL rules of procedure revealed no provision for mail ballots. As Jacobson observed, however, nothing in the document prohibited their use. And with no member of the DFL executive committee dissenting, a mail ballot was authorized and distributed. A tally of returned ballots gave overwhelming support to Jacobson's motion to remove Marsh as an endorsed candidate.

Marsh reacted angrily, gathering enough signatures on a petition to enter the DFL primary race for secretary of state without the party's endorsement. The DFL central committee endorsed Joseph Donovan, a Duluth resident.[14] Marsh failed to carry even his own precinct in the primary.[15]

Preparing for the 1954 Campaign

Humphrey earned a well-deserved reputation early in his political career for disorganized campaigns. Election-year 1954 was no exception. Preparations began almost 18 months before election day. In keeping with the circle-the-wagons strategy agreed to by Humphrey and the DFL leadership, the key leaders devoted their energies solely to the reelection of Hubert H. Humphrey to the U.S. Senate.

Humphrey had good reason to be concerned about 1954. A sense of despondency had fallen over the DFL leadership after the 1953 election.[16] Karl Rolvaag had served two years as party chair and would resign at the 1954 convention. The senator gave top priority initially to developing a statewide Humphrey volunteer organization, starting with a series of campaign schools in each congressional district. Various political leaders, including Freeman, served as "faculty."[17]

Humphrey had not designated a campaign manager. Instead, complaining to Freeman and other DFL officials that requests to speak at events in the state were interfering with the work of his Washington staff, Humphrey asked them to arrange speaking engagements through his Minnesota office.

Brushing aside Humphrey's ambivalence and his own conflict about a personal political future, Freeman devoted his energies in 1953 and early 1954 to Humphrey's reelection. The bruises of the 1952 campaign had healed by spring 1953, and Freeman plunged vigorously into the task. First, he wished to ensure the united and strong support of organized labor. With prompting from Gerald Heaney, he held a crucial meeting on June 14, 1953, near Duluth, with representatives of all the major unions in Minnesota.[18] Heaney readied for the meeting with a June 11 memo instructing Freeman to prepare an agenda: "If we do not have a program for discussion, I am afraid that very little will be accomplished."[19]

The agenda should include steps to "realize the full potential of the labor vote." Other than in presidential election years, Heaney noted, registration and other get-out-the-vote programs hadn't been successful. "I feel positive that we have only scratched the surface as to what can be done." Heaney said special emphasis was needed on labor in smaller cities as well as in Minneapolis, St. Paul, and Duluth and on the Iron Range.

"We must work on women's organizations, particularly in Minneapolis," he wrote. "You are probably sick and tired of hearing of my ideas, but [we know from] the last public opinion poll and from every other standard . . . that we haven't done a good job with women."

Heaney wrote of the need for recruiting strong congressional candidates, especially in Minnesota's Fifth and Seventh Districts. The candidates must enter the field immediately, financial assistance arranged. And, Heaney concluded, Humphrey needed a public-relations person, part time for the remainder of 1953 and full time in 1954.

Twenty-five people—including Humphrey, Freeman, Heaney, and Karl Rolvaag—attended the June 14 meeting outside Duluth.

"Minnesota Labor's League for Political Action" represented the American Federation of Labor (AFL). Roy Reuther, director of the Congress of Industrial Organizations (CIO), attended with other regional union officials. Karl Rolvaag, state DFL chair, opened the meeting, explaining that the DFL wanted to develop a program for labor's participation in the 1954 campaign for Humphrey's reelection. He said the party was arranging similar meetings with farm and cooperative leaders. Then he asked Freeman to speak.

Following Heaney's recommendation, Freeman began a discussion on women voters.[20] What had the unions done among the wives of organized labor? What plans were they making? An extended exchange on women in politics followed. The CIO had researched the issue extensively, Reuther said, noting that women accounted for 55 percent of the vote cast in the 1952 presidential election. He said about 70 percent of labor had voted for Stevenson.

Wives had voted the same as husbands in Detroit, but the union's research had not found the same relationship among labor couples elsewhere, Reuther said. The AFL leadership had coolly received efforts to emphasize women voters, said Jim McDevitt, Minnesota AFL president. But he reported that the union had established a women's division with a director and staff and warned against running union activities for women as an auxiliary.

Heaney intervened, shifting the discussion to a get-out-the-vote campaign for Humphrey. He said organized labor had had more than a dozen people working full time a year before the 1948 election. He introduced Humphrey, who commended Minnesota unions for their support six years earlier and outlined the most effective use of labor support before the November 1954 election.

Before the meeting could fall into a commentary on Humphrey's presentation, Heaney introduced the idea of a meeting in May 1953 to discuss the 1954 elections: "We cannot wait until summer of 1954 to begin work." Reuther had come prepared. He responded first by proposing a small, top-level committee organized to operate in close liaison with the DFL and to coordinate political activity with other joint labor committees in Minnesota communities. After several minutes of discussion on organizing procedures, informal versus formal status, and whether the Duluth meeting sufficiently represented organized labor, the 25 men agreed to the Reuther proposal. The meeting complete, they enjoyed a luncheon prepared by three women of Duluth.

"I think we have gotten some long-range programs underway here [that] can be very useful in planning steps [that] are to come," Freeman wrote to Humphrey shortly after the Duluth meeting.[21] Assuring the senator that details in implementing the Duluth agreement with labor were being worked out, Freeman asked Humphrey's advice on handling political attacks. Similar sniping constantly upset Humphrey. Freeman said some people advised party leaders to lash back immediately while others counseled them to ignore the attacks.

"Attack by some of *us* would have a deterring effect," Freeman said, summarizing the arguments. But "I wonder if the contrary isn't actually the case." He continued:

I was never happier than when someone challenged the statements that I made, with the resulting opportunity . . . to continue the interchange as long as the papers would pay it any heed. It is my best judgment that your continued trips back here is the best possible campaign. All reports I have received indicate that you are doing very well, and that the Republicans are pessimistic about their chances.

Freeman organized a "Kitchen Cabinet" in August 1953, to coordinate planning for Senator Humphrey's reelection campaign.[22] Although Karl Rolvaag was a member of the cabinet and remained chair of the state DFL, Freeman had assumed the function of campaign manager for the 1954 election. Two decisions emerged from the August meeting. First, the party organized a campaign staff for the senator's reelection. John Bystrom, an associate professor at the University of Minnesota, became office manager for his campaign. Humphrey, attending the meeting with two key members of his personal staff, informed his Minnesota office staff of the arrangement.

Second, the DFL state convention organized around Humphrey's reelection campaign. The party asked Bystrom to coordinate Humphrey's campaign activities with Freeman and the Kitchen Cabinet. The DFL executive committee and key DFL officials around the state got a chance to review the decision.

The Campaign

After the convention, Freeman pleaded with Humphrey to discuss with him the imminent campaign. Freeman's position was awkward. He was now the senator's running mate, no longer his putative campaign manager. But Freeman could hardly keep his take-charge nature from asserting itself. "I don't want to push you in any way on this or anything else. And I will most certainly keep out from under foot so far as your planning is concerned if you think that would be the most advantageous," he wrote. "I honestly want to fit into this where it will work the best for you. My main purpose in this campaign is to make a contribution to your victory."[23]

From Humphrey's perspective, the letter came from one who six months earlier had organized a circle-the-wagons campaign to focus on the senator's reelection, but who approached it now as a DFL campaign that would also elect Freeman governor. Freeman had been instrumental in obtaining a strong commitment from organized labor, and he clearly was in charge of the revitalized Minnesota DFL. The state DFL convention in Albert Lea had drawn more than 2,000 party members. It was, according to Freeman, "one of the experiences that lives in one's heart for a long time."[24]

Freeman pleaded again on April 15 for a meeting with Humphrey, noting that his own campaign schedule was filling up. "Will you give me an idea when would be a good time in terms of scheduling and also the crystallization of your plans?"

Humphrey replied on April 19, somewhat exasperated:

I am 1,200 miles away, trying to work long distance and to sandwich in a few minutes just to think what we can do. I will depend on you, I trust you and I respect your judgment. I think we will save a lot of time and trouble if we will center our contacts through specified people. My contact in Minnesota is Mitch Perrazo.

The carefully crafted plan to ensure coordination between the DFL and the Humphrey campaign was breaking down.[25]

On April 29, Humphrey urged Freeman to attack Val Bjornson, indeed the senator's Republican opponent that year.[26] "I have full faith and confidence in you to do what is right. You can't check with me on all these matters, nor need you. You know these issues as well as I do and I know you can handle them in a first-class manner."

The DFL emerged from its state convention with a strong ticket and a campaign strategy initially organized around Humphrey's reelection but enlarged to accommodate a statewide DFL ticket. It had enlisted the strong support of farmers, cooperatives, and labor organizations, as well as new methods and technologies to achieve maximum impact from a rather small budget. From Humphrey's perspective, an energized party organization, and a candidate for governor who was convinced he could win, may not have been the way to focus on the senatorial campaign, though it could achieve his purposes. Nor did it hurt that Val Bjornson, the Republican candidate, was an ineffective campaigner, as the polls demonstrated.

Freeman organized a DFL campaign office in Minneapolis that provided space for the campaign staff of all statewide DFL candidates. Humphrey, however, opened a separate campaign office. The task of coordinating the activities of the two campaigns fell to Tom Hughes, Freeman's campaign staff director, and Mitch Perrazo, head of Humphrey's Minnesota office. Bill Kubicek was the nominal campaign manager. John Bystrom continued as campaign director. But Freeman was effectively the manager of the campaign for governor and for the DFL.

The campaign repeated its central theme—"It's time for a change"—in many variations, most insistently in radio commercials of three to five minutes that opened with the ringing of an old-fashioned alarm clock, then a voice rasping the phrase "Wake up, Minnesota." The message reflected both the conviction of Freeman that his opponent and Republicans as a whole were ignoring social needs and public services and his frustration that the public did not seem to share his concerns. Newspaper ads carried headlines that "Minnesota Needs a Wide-Awake Governor," a winkish play on Governor Anderson's drooping eyelids.[27]

Freeman typically maintained a schedule of campaign appearances in five cities and towns per day in which he criticized the "paper curtain around the Capitol where Anderson is hiding in a shroud of silence." His stump speeches charged that mental-health programs were running down, derided conservation programs as a "hideous" mess, and declared that education and highway programs were "drifting aimlessly."[28] The DFL message that Anderson was not in control of state government gained some traction in page-one newspaper articles when Frank Pasternak, an escapee from the state prison at Stillwater, offered to surrender to Miles Lord, DFL candidate for attorney general. Pasternak said he wanted to tell about the prison conditions that two weeks earlier had led to a four-day riot.[29]

The *Minneapolis Star* and *Minneapolis Tribune* announced they would begin intensive election coverage two weeks before the election. But they found it hard to distract voters from other events on the national scene or at home. Marilyn Monroe married baseball legend Joe DiMaggio in late October.[30] Minneapolis was launching the economic revolution that changed American suburbs when the Daytons broke ground on October 29, 1954, for Southdale, the first enclosed shopping mall in America.[31] The U.S. Department of Agriculture announced a record harvest of feed grain, giving pessimistic readers the opportunity to worry that emerging economic patterns would plague farmers and rural communities for the rest of the century.[32]

As election day drew near, Freeman and Lord undertook a coordinated two-step tactic on campaign issues. Lord raised an issue and questioned the competence of Governor Anderson's administration. Freeman followed several days later, repeating the charge, then described how he would handle the matter. For example, the Department of Conservation had faced shortages in funds collected by county auditors for fish and game licenses, a problem revealed by a news story about losses in McLeod County. Lord said the commissioner of conservation was covering up a situation subsequently found in four other counties. The commissioner said he did not report the problem sooner because publicity would impede his investigation.[33]

Freeman picked up on the issue several days later, repeating his charge that the Anderson administration was "infected with creeping do-nothingism." Progress, he said, was possible "only if directed by men of ability and courage." He proposed a long-term conservation program to be developed by an advisory committee of citizens, experts, and sportsmen, appointed by the governor.[34]

Anderson's strategy was to ride above the political tempest. He met for lunch with the heads of state departments, spoke at the 30th anniversary of WCCO radio at a Minneapolis Athletic Club reception, and flew to Red Wing in a helicopter for a political tour.[35] Lord made his life miserable by alleging that the Anderson administration had conspired to purchase a St. Paul building as a state office annex "from prominent Republicans." The charge grew legs when the press reported that the chair of the House appropriations committee, a prominent Republican, was listed as the appraiser for the purchase. An angry Anderson replied that "the DFL smear mill was grinding out half-truths and innuendoes while I was attending church."[36] When the governor refused to launch an investigation, Freeman criticized him again for ignoring the problem

By the end of October, the campaign had become a contest of contrasting views about whether Minnesota voters should look to the future or the past. Anderson shifted his strategy of ignoring Freeman and the DFL campaigners to attack the "DFL ancestry of graft, corruption, payroll padding, contract favoritism, and other practices contrary to public good." Anderson explained his eagerness to revive campaign symbols of prewar Minnesota politics by saying, "I have had enough of this effort to smear my administration and myself."[37] Others stirred the pot of "fearing the past." P. Kenneth Peterson, the GOP candidate for lieutenant governor, had telegraphed GOP tactics earlier in a more pointed personal attack on Freeman. He charged that "Freeman would return to an administration that only 16 years ago proved to be so corrupt and boss ridden [that] the people of Minnesota threw them out of office."[38] Stafford King, running for reelection as the GOP candidate for state auditor, may have confused voters by appearing to exclude Democrats when he charged that "the Farmer-Labor Party ran Minnesota government into the red, increased state debt, raised property taxes higher than ever before." Patting himself on the back, King said, "The GOP changed all that. We have surpluses today in all state funds."[39]

Freeman and the DFL pounded hard on raising voter doubts about whether Minnesota was preparing adequately for the future. "A flood of children headed toward public schools over eight years ago, but the GOP had no response: no plans formulated, no policies initiated, no legislation passed," Freeman said. "If the DFL wins, I'll tell you what I will do: I will give executive direction both in the state administration and in the legislature."[40]

As the campaign entered its final days, the Minneapolis papers said Governor Anderson "deserved reelection because of his record." The editorial writer said Freeman "is an honest and able man but has no administrative background and experience."[41] The editorial pages also endorsed Bjornson, who "will make a first-rate Senator."[42] That same day the Minnesota Poll predicted Anderson's reelection with 53 percent of the vote over Freeman and Humphrey's defeat of Bjornson with 56 percent.[43]

Freeman believed an event occurring on Saturday, November 1, three days before the election, tipped the balance in his favor. He was returning home in the waning days of the campaign, facing the news of a *Minneapolis Tribune* poll to be published Sunday indicating that he was running behind. After stopping for gas, his driver returned to the car with a Republican leaflet being placed under the windshield wipers of cars nearby. The last-minute leaflet carried a photograph of three dead Marines floating on the beach at the invasion of Tarawa during the South Pacific campaign in World War II. The caption read "Democrats Cause Wars."

"I was so outraged I could not speak," Freeman recalled. "During my short political career I had never said a word about my experiences in the war or about being seriously wounded. Now I was confronted with a leaflet in which Republican candidates were literally using the bodies of dead American soldiers to score a few points in the election. I was going home to rest but instead returned to campaign headquarters and went to work with a sense of rage."[44]

His anger fueled by pride as a veteran U.S. Marine, Freeman scheduled a half-hour telecast, appearing only with family and friends, two days before the election. The leaflet was a fumbled attack on Humphrey, deferred from active duty in World War II. But Humphrey was reluctant to appear with Freeman on the issue on a Sunday evening. Focusing on Freeman the veteran, the embodiment of the war issue, heightened the effectiveness of the live telecast. Freeman's mother unexpectedly pointed out, with great effect, that the scars on his face were from wounds taken in fighting on Bougainville as he defended his country.[45] Freeman vented his outrage in a statement praising the heroism of those who died in action. Holding the Republican leaflet, he condemned the attempt to introduce the deaths of U.S. Marines into a political campaign. The program, following Ed Sullivan's popular *Toast of the Town,* garnered an estimated 500,000 viewers.

The next day, Monday, a statewide DFL telecast from ten television stations blanketed all but the northwestern counties of Minnesota. The Republican campaign planners were not able to duplicate the feat in the 1954 election. By 1956, no station would agree to participate in a statewide television blackout for a political campaign.

The DFL ticket swept to victory on election day, November 4, 1954. Freeman received 52 percent of the vote, to become the first DFL governor elected in Minnesota. All but one DFL-endorsed candidate won on the races for state office. Miles Lord was elected attorney general, Joseph Donovan secretary of state, Karl Rolvaag lieutenant governor, and Arthur Hanson state treasurer. Only Stafford King among the Republican office-holders survived—he became state auditor by a close margin. Five of the nine DFL candidates for the U.S. House of Representatives succeeded, and Humphrey returned to the U.S. Senate for a second term.

Sifting through the election returns to find reason for the DFL sweep, political analysts reached several conclusions, all suggesting the DFL campaign superior in its tactics and objectives. Wallace Mitchell, the political reporter for the *Minneapolis Star,* credited Freeman's strength in counties along Minnesota's southern border. There the GOP did not receive the normally large margins necessary to offset DFL votes on the Iron Range and in St. Paul. Freeman had campaigned extensively in those areas, attacking the Republican farm program.[46] The Minnesota Poll, in querying voters as to factors leading to the DFL victory, found that 29 percent of the Anderson voters believed he had lost the election because of farmer resentment over GOP policies. Among Freeman voters, in contrast, 25 percent credited a desire for change as the most important factor in the DFL win.[47] Political pundits, unaware of the consensus among Humphrey and the DFL leadership that Freeman could not win, generally credited Humphrey's star power with carrying the ticket to victory.

Fortunes change swiftly in politics. Less than two years earlier the DFL had been broke, ready to close its state office. In December 1954, members of the DFL central committee received a letter appointing them to the attendance committee for the inaugural ball. After a frustrating decade, the DFL had achieved its first objective—to build a critical political mass capable of winning elections.

Next came the tasks of building momentum, creating the capacity to educate, achieving status for the DFL as a political party, and isolating political opponents in a nonpartisan context. Freeman grasped the challenge with relish. His success or failure would determine the future of the DFL and set the direction of the state.

Freeman emerged from his 1956 campaign as political leader of the state and head of a vibrant DFL. On January 9, 1957, he acknowledged his family before delivering his second inaugural address. Behind him is Karl Rolvaag; Joe Donovan is at his side.

—*3*—

The 1956 Campaign

Governor-elect Orville L. Freeman and his wife, Jane, slipped away shortly after November 4, 1954, to spend a postelection vacation in Florida. If Jane Freeman had hopes for relaxation, they were quickly dashed. Lieutenant Governor-elect Karl Rolvaag and Attorney General-elect Miles Lord accompanied the Freemans.[1] Orville was already thinking about the 1956 election. Such anticipation, with subsequent planning and attention to detail, characterized his overall approach to the work of government.

The week in Florida, a welcome opportunity to shed the tensions of the campaign, began a series of discussions about the future of the newly elected state officials and the just-resuscitated Democratic-Farmer-Labor Party. The electees explored strategies for solidifying the DFL, determined the goals of the Freeman administration for the 1955 legislative session, and assessed ways to work with the legislature given that Rolvaag was to be president of the Senate. The trio especially explored how to neutralize Republican campaign rhetoric suggesting the DFL would plunge state government into crisis such as Minnesota had experienced 18 years earlier.

If anyone took notes on their conversations, none of the notes has survived. If Freeman's actions upon their return to Minnesota are any guide, an outline would have included reopening the state budget proposal prepared under Gov. C. Elmer Anderson for presentation to the legislature in January. The new governor intended to submit the first DFL budget recommendations instead. He stressed political overtures to the business community, especially the banking, investment, manufacturing, and construction industries.

Freeman would plunge into a speaking schedule to describe DFL goals to citizen, educational, civic, and farm groups and associations. Most important, he would use symbolic occasions to convey his intention of taking charge of Minnesota government. Furthermore, he wished to instill a new sense of citizen participation in governance.

Neither Freeman nor his campaign staff had drawn up a master plan before his election; nor did time following that event allow such luxury. The realities of a two-year term were strict and brutal. The winning candidate must plan how to govern while strategizing for re-election. Often the provisions of the first task were indistinguishable from those of the second. Freeman had no doubt he would run again.

The good news was that voters usually gave first-term incumbents the benefit of a doubt. But Freeman had more to prove than most first-termers. The DFL's long trek in political wilderness was a constant reminder of the skepticism with which the Minnesota electorate viewed the ability of the DFLers to govern. Had the fires of the party's radicalism really died out? The DFL was an untested body of political volunteers entrusted with the powers of state government. That was all voters knew.

Freeman possessed several assets crucial to his success. The spasm of doubt following his defeat in the 1952 gubernatorial campaign had deepened his resolve. His victory in 1954 had tempered to a fine edge his conviction that success would be a reward for hard work, perseverance, and dedication. He was honing one essential characteristic of good managers: the ability to break goals into distinct tasks, to identify the work output necessary to achieve each task, and to bring together individual outcomes in a successful whole. He had a knack for recognizing individuals for their talents, and he was unusually persuasive with the people he wanted to join his effort. His greatest strength, many observers believed, was a unique ability to attract competent people and pull from them creative energy—sometimes exceeding their physical endurance.[2]

Among his first activities as governor-elect, Freeman paid a visit on November 14, 1954, to the organizing meeting of the 19 newly elected state senators of the Liberal minority Senate caucus. There he congratulated Don Fraser, first-term senator from Minneapolis's second precinct (Freeman's home precinct), upon his election as caucus secretary.[3] Two days later, exhibiting his sometime wry sense of humor, Freeman walked in unannounced on the 56 state senators attending the organizing meeting of the Conservative majority. After a flustered pause, the startled Conservatives invited Freeman in with a standing shower of applause.[4]

The most immediate task for the governor-elect was to find good people and persuade them to help run state government. Academic institutions, mostly those in and around the Twin Cities, provided a remarkable pool of skilled people from which to select advisors, staff, and agency executives. The people of Minnesota had sent their children to these schools, confident they would become capable of managing the public's business. The University of Minnesota was the crucible in which Freeman had shaped his concepts of governance. Countless hours of study and endless bull sessions with faculty and students had molded his views. Freeman and Hubert H. Humphrey were debating champions in 1939. Many faculty members had worked as volunteers in the DFL in the decade before Freeman's election in 1954. Now he offered an invitation to put words into action.

In his first appointment, Freeman chose Thomas R. Hughes, DFL secretary and longtime personal assistant, for his executive secretary. Hughes had taken two years from Minnesota politics in 1951 to serve in the U.S. Army during the Korean War, mostly in Japan. He had returned to Macalester College, where he was Minnesota oratorical champ in 1953. Hughes had been active in DFL politics since 1946. He was Freeman's alter ego.[5]

The two began to examine the state of the state government the next day. The first problem was an order by outgoing Governor Anderson to cut spending by 5 percent in the first six months of 1955 to counter an unexpected reduction in iron-ore tax revenues.[6] Freeman discussed the funding crisis with Earl Berg, Anderson's commissioner of administration, who suggested the governor-elect bring into pre-inaugural preparations his own designee for that position. Berg even offered to resign early, informing the governor-elect that Anderson was agreeable to the immediate appointment of Freeman's designee.[7] Two days later Freeman met with Governor Anderson to discuss the pending shortfall in iron-ore tax receipts as well as the administration post. The attorney general, Anderson said, had prepared a ruling that would authorize the governor to borrow against anticipated 1955 tax revenues to cover the prospective shortfall. The ruling would give state government access to $3 million and thus avert cutbacks in vital programs. Governor Anderson also said he would appoint Freeman's commissioner of administration as indicated.[8]

Although the selection of candidates to fill essential positions in the Freeman administration already was underway, the designation of commissioner of administration now took on urgency. The title inadequately describes a position with equivalent power to that of a deputy governor. Freeman's search reached across the Atlantic to Europe, paused briefly in Washington, D.C., and settled in the University of Minnesota. There he consulted with Lloyd Short, chair of the political science department and his predecessor, William Anderson, as well as with LeRoy Harlow, chair of the Minnesota Little Hoover Commission on Government Reorganization. They recommended Arthur Naftalin, associate professor of political science at the university.[9] Naftalin had been secretary to the mayor of Minneapolis during Humphrey's term in 1944–48. He was the archetype of the brilliant individuals Freeman brought into state government. And he contributed significantly to the quality and rise of Minnesota liberalism.

The commissioner of administration provides pivotal management in the operation of state government agencies. The office directly controls the purse strings by awarding contracts for maintenance, repair, and construction of state buildings and by recommending spending requests for state agencies to the governor for inclusion in the state budget. Each state agency must make a compelling case to the commissioner every two years for the appropriations requested by the governor from the legislature. Each must prepare to defend increases in spending over previously approved levels. The commissioner may and often does reduce spending requests. Agency heads may appeal such decisions during budget reviews by the governor. But every agency head, aware that challenging the commissioner risks incurring future wrath, prefers to maintain friendly relations.

The commissioner also functions as an early warning system for major problems in an agency. He or she must intercede early in suggesting or imposing adjustments in management policies or personnel. The worst criticism to befall a commissioner of administration is that he has failed to alert the governor to stage-agency management issues that might trigger political problems. A king must not be surprised; neither must a governor.

In keeping with his commitment to Freeman, Governor Anderson announced on November 23 that he would immediately appoint Naftalin as acting commissioner of administration, giving Naftalin authority to plan the transition of government during the next 60 days.[10] This afforded the time Freeman needed to draw up a plan.

Freeman's second priority was to remake the biennial budget. Traditionally, the retiring governor supervises preparation of the budget, a process starting early in an election year and largely completed a month before the November election. If the incoming governor is new, his administration might tweak the figures for political effect but not normally make major changes. So the first budget that a new governor submits to the legislature generally reflects the handiwork of his predecessor. Now Naftalin's first assignment was to prepare a new budget.

Freeman recruited Walter Heller, a professor of economics at the university who considered involvement in the political process an obligation, to work on this task with Naftalin.[11] The work was physically daunting and emotionally draining, enough so that Heller was hospitalized for a week after wrapping up the new budget. Freeman was not prepared to accept the priorities of the retiring Gov. C. Elmer Anderson as spending proposals for 1957 and 1958. Instead, an intense effort to reset funding priorities provided significant administrative, organizational, and political values:

- The budget proposal must convey to voters that the new DFL administration was not content with the status quo and would spare no effort to develop postwar proposals based on fresh appraisal of the need for state services.
- The budget proposal must be consistent with the future policy direction of the DFL. Naftalin, Heller, and Freeman were aware that the real goals and priorities of any agency or government are revealed in the details of the budget. Legislative leaders, the press, the business community, and social service advocates would study it to determine Freeman's political objectives, regardless of DFL rhetoric.
- The budget-proposal process must increase his own knowledge and give him experience in state government. Freeman

was a hands-on manager. He wanted to understand the functions of agencies so as to evaluate the qualifications of the individuals from whom he would select to manage programs. In the month-long period before inauguration, during which Naftalin and Heller held budget hearings with the staff of state agencies, Freeman sat in on most of the hearings, going to school on the details of Minnesota government. Here he gained a comprehensive working knowledge of agency operations and assessed the capabilities of those administering the services of the state.

Two weeks after returning from the week's vacation in Florida, Freeman worked from a small transition office in the Minnesota State Capitol, usually from 7 A.M. until after midnight.[12] Without official status or funds, he already had assembled an informal cabinet of advisors. They included George Selke, former president of what is now St. Cloud State University, on education; Frank Rarig, secretary of the Wilder Foundation, on welfare; Byron G. Allen, national Democratic committeeman; Joe Robbie, future DFL Fifth District congressional candidate, on political issues; Karl Grittner, then a state representative, on election-law revisions; David Winton, board chairman of Winton Lumber, on business; and Orlin Folwick of the Minnesota Federation of Labor, on labor policy.

Freeman told reporters on November 30, 1955, that he would appoint Dorothy M. Jacobson, assistant professor of political science at Macalester College, as his personal assistant.[13] Jacobson took a leave of absence from Macalester to write speeches, prepare messages, and serve as staff liaison in the governor's office. She never returned to academic life. Her first task was to draft Freeman's inaugural message.

Other appointments followed in December. Naftalin needed reliable numbers for developing tax-revenue projections, which meant a trustworthy expert to calculate budget numbers. On Heller's recommendation, he drafted Joseph Robertson, tax specialist in the Department of Taxation, to work on the new budget. Soon after inauguration, Freeman appointed Robertson commissioner of the department, vaulting him over several levels of superiors.[14] Morrie Hursh, a nationally recognized expert in welfare policy, was working in Wisconsin when Freeman named him commissioner of welfare.[15] Freeman appointed George Selke, former president of St. Cloud State Teachers College and of the University of Montana, the commissioner of the Department of Natural Resources.[16] Eugenie Anderson, whom President Truman had appointed U.S. ambassador to Denmark, would head up the new Fair Employment Practices Commission that Freeman proposed and the legislature authorized in 1955.

Freeman used the office of governor in the pre-inaugural months of 1954 to shape public perceptions of the incoming administration and the DFL. One of his first actions was to travel to New York's Wall Street to extol the virtues of Minnesota as a place in which to invest and locate companies. The DFL had exploded into national prominence in 1954, not only by returning Humphrey easily to the U.S. Senate but also by sweeping in all but one nominee for state office and gaining 19 seats in the Minnesota House of Representatives. This was its first majority (by one) in the House since 1937. The DFL gained two congressional seats to give the party a five-to-four edge in the state's delegation to the U.S. House of Representatives. Minnesota was a political anomaly, a hyphenated Democratic state floating in a midwestern sea of Republican governors.[17] The eastern centers of money and political power were curious: Was the DFL more than a new political party? Was it a harbinger of political change in middle America?

Freeman seized the opportunity to display before the New York investment community the politician dismissed in 1953 as a 36-year-old-has-been but now at the head of a rising political party. He also used the New York visit to dampen speculation about the economic policies of the DFL. Freeman described Minnesota as a place of good, stable government, with a highly educated workforce and healthy environment offering expansive outdoor recreational opportunities. He said he believed social gains must come with the help of government and that tax dollars spent on good schools, better health services, conservation, and roads and highways were an investment in the future. Wall Street was the perfect platform from which to speak to Minnesota and its citizens. His appearance established that the new governor would listen to the business community. It provided him the opportunity to speak early for all Minnesotans, and it inoculated both the governor and the DFL against sniping by members of the GOP or the business community.

Freeman was inaugurated January 4, 1955, as the 29th governor of Minnesota. He plunged with gusto into a vigorous three-month legislative session. The DFL had become the majority caucus by one vote in the House of Representatives. The DFL minority in the Senate was small but effective. Freeman proposed to increase state funding for per-pupil-assistance to public schools, fulfilling a campaign pledge. The legislature readily adopted his proposal for major improvements in welfare services. He also requested higher old-age-assistance payments, the easing of disability restrictions, and the broadening of vocational rehabilitation. He proposed more beds in state hospitals for mental and alcoholic patients. The legislature made only minor changes to his budget. He suggested new programs in conservation and agriculture, which the legislature also approved. Freeman proposed and the legislature agreed to submit for voter approval in 1956 a program for highway-user fund distributions. And, to pay for increases in school assistance, it would ask voters in 1956 to approve a shift of current iron-ore tax receipts from a quarter-billion-dollar trust fund into general revenues for current school use.[18]

Recognizing his debt to organized labor for its political support, Freeman proposed and the legislature raised unemployment and workers-compensation benefits. Workers gained relief from individual liability in labor disputes through the removal of an onerous provision used by companies to intimidate striking workers that Gov. Harold Stassen had proposed in the late 1930s. A Fair Employment Practices Act authorized the governor to appoint a commission and review panel. The commission gained authority to obtain court enforcement, where necessary, of orders outlawing discrimination by employers, employment agencies, or labor unions.

The 1955 session was the start of a six-year thrust-and-parry relationship with the Conservative leaders of the Minnesota Senate over tax policy.[19] With the aid of the DFL caucuses in state House and Senate, Freeman was able to move the legislature forward on environment and conservation, social policy, and education programs. Conservative members differed over the scope and pace of the programs but not with their direction.

The opponents of social programs had more subtly disguised their preferences in their approach to tax policy. If new taxes were necessary, the Conservatives and the members of the business community preferred a sales tax as the basic source of revenues. Freeman and the DFL strongly supported a graduated income tax based on the ability of Minnesotans to pay.[20] Twenty years earlier, the Minnesota legislature had adopted a graduated income tax proposed by Floyd B. Olson, the first Farmer-Labor governor, while rejecting a general sales tax.

Freeman recommended withholding through payroll deduction as a pay-as-you-go method of collecting taxes. He argued that withholding could eliminate revenue losses from nonpayment of taxes, which amounted in 1955 to an estimated $2 million underpayment. Conservatives strongly opposed withholding, for tactical and strategic reasons. The DFL victory in 1954 bespoke a shift in public attitudes toward the role of state government in providing programs and services and a willingness to support increases in tax revenues to pay for them.

As small-government advocates, Republicans believed the lump-sum payment of income taxes would remind voters of the cost of government each year, causing taxpayer resentment to grow into opposition to spending for public services. A $12 million loss in revenues yearly was a small price to pay. Republicans and the business advocates preferred a tax policy shifting the cost of government mainly to a sales tax, the most regressive form of taxation, without regard for ability to pay.

Freeman and the DFL adroitly used withholding as a symbol for the income tax. While only a means of tax collection, withholding conveys the perception that such a tax system is progressive, or equitable, as well as fair, because it prevents cheating. With political support for DFL policies on the rise, the Conservatives had no appetite for a head-to-head battle over withholding versus sales tax. Believing that announced intent to withhold would weaken chances for enactment of a sales tax, they chose a tax-policy menu combining delay with a touch of irresponsibility. Opposition to withholding would delay action on appropriations for programs that the Conservatives would support without proposing alternative revenue measures. Despite the constitutional requirement that sufficient revenue measures accompany spending proposals, the Conservatives hoped to force Freeman to propose a sales tax as the only alternative acceptable to the legislature.

The federal government had adopted withholding as a tax policy during World War II to ease the collection of higher income-tax revenues to pay for war. Adoption had been slow at the state level, and Minnesota was among the first states to propose adoption of the practice. As voters began to demand betters schools, roads, environmental programs, and health-and-welfare systems—all programs for which the state provides funding—a rise in tax revenues was inevitable. The DFL believed taxes should derive from wages, salaries, and investments. Those with higher incomes and thus more disposable income could afford to pay more than low-income families and households. If the public supported more services, then the role of government was to ensure the equity of the system, the relative ease of the burden of payment, and the punishment of cheaters. Withholding had obvious public appeal as a way to infuse fairness in the tax system.

But withholding also had a dark side, one its advocates were sometimes loath to acknowledge. Putting withholding into practice would double income taxes in the first year. The taxpayer, already liable for taxes on wages earned the previous year, would take a cut in current income through deductions for taxes due the next. The additional tax revenues would provide a one-time windfall. Any part of a windfall retained to finance programs would constitute a one-year increase. Freeman proposed to pay for the new programs with a portion of the windfall and return the rest as a refund.

After a protracted legislative fight in 1955, Freeman and the DFL leaders cobbled together a tax package to gain Conservative support and provide increased spending for education, social programs, and the environment. Withholding was dropped in favor of increased revenues from a series of excise taxes (a selective use of the sales tax). Political realities led Freeman to declare victory for the DFL and his administration.[21] He had achieved his major objectives. Withholding was put aside for another legislative session, and he turned his attention to the 1956 election.

The DFL sweep of 1954 had stunned Minnesota Republicans as well as the press in Minnesota and political observers outside the state. Freeman's performance during his first term further surprised and impressed the state's editorial writers.[22] Republican leaders examining the 1956 campaign could not be optimistic about the future. Party strategists, looking beyond the next two years, worried about GOP Sen. Edward J. Thye, a one-term former governor, who sought reelection in 1958. The elections in 1954 had demonstrated that the Republicans could offer little viable political leadership. Strong candidates were scarce. Examining GOP prospects for the 1956 campaign, *Minneapolis Tribune* political writer Rolf Felstad speculated at the end of 1954 that "Anderson could come back." He had won seven of nine statewide campaigns going back to 1940. Felstad listed other potential candidates, including Val Bjornson, Stafford King, Rep. Walter Judd, future chief justice of the U.S. Supreme Court Warren Burger (a St. Paul attorney then working in the Justice Department), P. Kenneth Peterson (GOP candidate for lieutenant governor), and state representative Jon Hartle (GOP state chair). If the Republicans could not recapture the political initiative in 1956, the party faced a gloomy and uncertain future in Minnesota.

"Much depends, they concede, on what kind of record Freeman can construct, particularly in the 1955 legislative session," Felstad wrote, eerily predicting the outcome Freeman sought and achieved—and the Republicans' worst dream scenario.

Small wonder, then, that none of the potential GOP gubernatorial candidates of 1954 was able to secure the Republican nomination for governor in 1956. The Republicans had one potentially enormous asset, however. President Dwight D. Eisenhower would head up the 1956 GOP national campaign in his bid for reelection. And he had led the Minnesota GOP to a sweep of state offices in 1952. As the DFL had made Humphrey its star attraction in 1954, so would the GOP make Eisenhower—"Ike"—the centerpiece of its 1956 campaign. To make the linkage clear, the Republicans brought Ancher Nelsen, a likeable Minnesota Republican, back from Washington, D.C., to run against Freeman. Nelsen was serving as Eisenhower's director of the Rural Electrification Administration (REA). The highly popular agency in the Department of Agriculture, born of the Roosevelt New Deal, brought electric power to rural Minnesota with low-interest development loans. It spawned dozens of rural electric cooperatives, each with a board of directors keenly aware of the importance of politics in funding the agency. The political irony of a Republican candidate looking to run on the reflected luster of a program of Democratic progeny did not faze the Minnesota GOP.

Freeman, the engineer of the 1954 DFL sweep, would head the DFL ticket. Humphrey had been the star two years earlier, but now Freeman and the other DFL leaders faced the test: Could they continue to change the political character and reshape the politics of Minnesota?

Bill Kubicek coordinated the 1956 campaign. John Bystrom, whose mastery of detail and organization Humphrey's campaign staff had spurned, managed it. Walter F. (Fritz) Mondale, a recent graduate of the University of Minnesota Law School who had coordinated Freeman's appearances outside plant gates in 1954, was the associate campaign coordinator.[23] The DFL established its central campaign office with space and staff for all its candidates for state office. Organized labor secured a separate political-action campaign group to support the DFL ticket, much as it had in 1954. A DFL campaign office opened on the Iron Range under the direction of Gerald Heaney. Ray Hemenway, DFL chair, and Ann Vetter, cochair, coordinated DFL county activities, primarily to help organize Freeman's outstate appearances. Tom Hughes sat at the center of the network, making decisions for Freeman in his absence, a frequent situation with the governor constantly traveling the state.

The organization of the campaign may have seemed confused and disorganized to outsiders, but appearances were deceptive. Every campaign is hectic and confusing. The principals of the several staff groups involved in a campaign do not have the luxury of negotiation. Communications have one function—to ensure prompt action. But all of the key figures in the 1956 election had been together since 1948. They were practiced in working amid the disarray of campaign life. The leadership group operated with a high level of trust. Its 1956 meetings did not involve negotiations over assignments or strategy. Rather, meetings and conferences turned to coordination, how to execute the reelection plan in a timely manner, how to correct immediate problems.

Campaign planning initially focused on two organizational guidelines: First, DFL candidates must run as a ticket, with state office, congressional, and legislative districts candidates appearing on sample ballots. Second, TV and radio, building on party successes with television two years earlier, must be the primary means of reaching Minnesota voters.

The campaign adopted a third, unspoken, guideline after the 1956 primary elections in September. While the Republicans built their campaign in Minnesota around President Eisenhower, the DFL campaigned on state races and issues, with only minimal support for Adlai Stevenson, the Democratic presidential candidate.[24]

Freeman campaigned across Minnesota over the next year and a half, delivering up to eight speeches a day in a schedule bringing him into every county at least once. The speeches meant to establish a sense of confidence in the new governor and government. Government enabled individuals to organize programs to attack problems beyond the capacity of one person or community to solve. As a quarterback on the University of Minnesota football team, Freeman had learned that winning was a team effort directing individual skills toward explicit goals. As a combat officer he quickly understood that survival involved the organized effort of a squad of individuals, each dependent on the other to achieve specific objectives.

Political leadership is a skill. A political leader organizes and focuses the potential of individuals with different abilities and of institutions with different interests to achieve a specific goal. The goal at hand was to convince voters they could produce measurable achievements in education, welfare, transportation, conservation, and other public goals through political action. The campaign for reelection in 1956 sought to make the case that the DFL was a means to plan and organize state government to reach shared goals. The campaign gave

DFL members an opportunity to provide leadership in their own communities supporting the goals of programs proposed by the new governor.

"Minnesota Builds" (with the DFL) became a campaign theme, a slogan based on tangible evidence. In reviewing Anderson's 1955 budget recommendations, Naftalin and Freeman had discovered that spending proposals for capital equipment—that is for state colleges and the University of Minnesota as well as state hospitals, correctional institutions, parks, and other recreational facilities—did not cover the estimated cost of maintenance, let alone any new buildings or facilities.[25]

Completing a new survey of building and maintenance needs was impossible in the two months before the 1955–57 budget went to the legislature. Freeman proposed the establishment of a special legislative committee to prepare recommendations on capital spending for the 1957 session. When Naftalin presented the details of the deteriorating status of buildings and facilities to the House and Senate committees in 1955, state legislators created a committee on state building needs—and named Naftalin a voting member and its chair.

The action of the 1955 legislature was unique in breaking down the walls of political power and underscored the crisis for state facilities. Separation of executive and legislative powers in government is a constitutional feature of American democracy, and each branch of government is zealous in guarding its authority. Rarely, if ever, does one branch share its constitutional power with another. The authority to appropriate—to determine the spending of public funds—is uniquely a legislative responsibility. In this instance, however, the legislature named the top management official of the executive branch as chair of a key legislative committee equally divided between House and Senate. The legislature, in effect, gave the governor the deciding vote on the amount and pace of spending for the modernization of public buildings.[26]

Naftalin quickly put his unique authority to work, organizing the legislative committee's visits to the University of Minnesota, all state colleges (now part of Minnesota State Colleges and Universities, or MNSCU), state hospitals and mental institutions, state prisons, and key conservation facilities. The committee during 1955 and 1956 traveled throughout the state to examine office and workspace facilities for state agencies, to review reports of maintenance needs, and to discuss options for updating record keeping and reporting in state licensing operations.

The Naftalin committee conducted its assessment of capital-equipment requirements for Minnesota at the same time Freeman campaigned for reelection. When he spoke about the opportunity to "Build Minnesota," many if not most legislators knew he was talking about repairing and enlarging the infrastructure of public services in the state. Subsequently (in 1957), Freeman proposed and the legislature approved a capital budget of $50 million, the largest in Minnesota history.

A New Campaign Model

Early in 1956 a new campaign model began to evolve. As in 1954, volunteers largely staffed the campaign with only a few paid specialists. John W. Bystrom, formerly assigned to run Sen. Hubert Humphrey's 1954 reelection, became overall campaign manager for 1956. Like many of the key political volunteers, Bystrom was an academic, an assistant professor in education on leave from the University of Minnesota.

"Freeman is in the center of his own campaign, thoroughly cognizant of the situation," a campaign staffer asserted in 1956, "and in many ways is his own campaign manager."[27]

Bystrom segmented the campaign into specific activity areas, with volunteer organizers responsible for each segment. At the end of the campaign, each received a personal letter of thanks from Freeman, but only after his study of an extensive report describing achievements, examining problems, and recommending changes in procedures. All this in anticipation of the campaign two years hence.

Walter Mondale, as associate campaign manager in charge of suburban campaigning, plant-gate visits, and congressional-district tours, prepared an exhaustive analysis of his part in the 1956 campaigns. Mondale's report captured both the precision and frustration of the campaign:

> Freeman himself should be content with tours which are not perfect technical accomplishments. Tours are imprecise at best; the attempt to achieve too much in technical perfection probably takes additional energy better spent elsewhere. Also, when Freeman gets steamed up over a technical problem, the local committee and audience senses it, and his visit loses some of the warmth that is important.

Mondale's report on congressional district tours is a manual for organizing and managing campaign tours, applicable today with only minor updating. For example, Mondale made this recommendation:

> The person who plans the tours should also go along and be in charge of them. (Which probably means that he can't be expected to do much else if there is a heavy tour schedule, as was the case this year.) This is the best guarantee of a smooth working schedule.

The same precision is evident in other reports. Marge Maki, a party activist from St. Louis Park, was in charge of organizing suburban coffee parties for women, a DFL experiment. Traditional methods, especially the political rallies that had been a Democratic and Farmer-Labor mainstay in prewar campaigning, fell flat in the suburbs. Like the Tupperware parties used to reach women in postwar suburban developments, coffee parties allowed the DFL to take advantage of one of its greatest strengths—women on the campaign trail, particularly the wives of the candidates.

"At first," Maki wrote in her report, "the 9:30 A.M. time seemed too ghastly—but [it proved] the most popular and effective hour. All but one at this hour had 22 or more people at it." From there, she proceeded:

> About hostesses. Generally speaking, our old regulars did not respond too well in this program. Few agreed to have one— and most [of the] time when they did, the parties were smaller and less enthusiastic. New precinct people were the best. The best hostesses are those active in other civic affairs.
>
> To be really effective, this project needs a woman in each ward who has a wide acquaintance in other fields, who has unlimited patience with women who can't make up their minds—or can sell the idea over the phone—and enough perseverance to make approximately 24 phone calls of varying lengths to fill one day of parties. (Believe it or not, I found some women like this).
>
> The biggest part of this type of campaigning is the follow-up. These women *must* be contacted again for some future activity to get their interest.
>
> Some thought should be given by Jane [Freeman], Florence [Rolvaag], et al., to setting up a day a month for coffee parties in the suburbs. This is one really effective answer to our suburban problem—but adds to theirs. Maybe two or three parties could be held in one afternoon.
>
> Finally, the guys who were elected should give a big bow to their wives on this project. After going to 55 parties with them, no one knows better than I how hard these girls

worked. No matter how tired, how miserable the weather, how sick they were of fancy desserts and coffee, they sparkled and charmed. (Some of the darndest old bags fell their victims, believe me.) I like their husbands—but I loved the wives.

Maki's report, a manual for organizing women volunteers, is but one example of the role of volunteers in the emergence of the DFL as the dominant political force in Minnesota.

Aaron Litman, a St. Paul newspaperman, and Jim Tintner, a young volunteer, were responsible for developing press releases and coordinating press activities with those of other statewide candidates. Both conceded it was a miserable job.[28] St. Paul consultant Sheldon Goldstein managed television programming, a series of ten-, 15-, and 30-minute recorded and live programs providing the informational backbone of the campaign. Paul Cashman, a Minneapolis radio consultant and one of the few paid campaign staffers, did the bulk of the writing, producing, and scheduling of mostly five-minute radio programs recorded by Freeman. Educational in nature, with minimal partisan content, the radio programs highly frustrated Republican strategists. The GOP scheduled time for rebuttal after each program, but the Republican candidates sounded angry and petulant in their responses as Freeman gave them little to criticize.[29] And he never mentioned Ancher Nelsen, his opponent. In a typical week, Freeman spoke from 81 different radio spots. Between October 13 and November 6, the campaign purchased station time for 19 TV programs; 16 were telecast live because programs recorded by kinescope were of poor technical quality.

The written reports are the first cohesive, comprehensive record for coordinated statewide DFL campaigns. They represent the basic blueprint for the modern postwar political campaigns in Minnesota.[30] Reliance on television, particularly on the statewide telecast of single political events, debuted in 1954 along with the sample ballot. A powerful instrument, the sample ballot identified candidates endorsed at DFL caucuses, congressional-district conventions, and state DFL conventions. Statewide DFL candidates ran as a ticket, another innovation, and provided visibility for candidates for local government and state legislative offices. The final and probably the most important DFL innovation was the development of the campaign blueprint for managing statewide political campaigns.

John Bystrom prepared as one of the last memos of the 1956 campaign a report detailing its cost. He calculated that campaign expenditures amounted to about $124,000, including labor and the cost for TV and radio time.[31] The development of campaign blueprints that spell out tactical objectives and strategic goals, combined with a thorough analysis of the reasons for success or failure, might be a valuable historical memory for future campaign planners and strategists. Unfortunately, the DFL has neither maintained these documents as a resource nor built a historical record from subsequent campaigns. While its reliance on volunteers explains the rise of the DFL to prominence, the weakness of such a movement lies in its inability to recall its past, an asset that political professionals prize.

The 1956 Campaign

As September drew to a close, the GOP and DFL campaigns came slowly into focus. Ancher Nelsen, the GOP gubernatorial candidate, chided Freeman for remaining silent on a remark by Estes Kefauver, vice-presidential candidate on the national Democratic ticket. Supposedly Kefauver had disparaged the Rural Electric Administration (REA), from which Nelsen had resigned to run for governor.[32] Freeman was the lightning rod for the GOP ticket. Val Bjornson, wrapping up a three-day GOP rally on the Iron Range, berated Freeman in Duluth for calling a tax levy on every adult Minnesotan a "GOP head tax." "Everyone in the legislature voted for it," Bjornson, the GOP candidate for state treasurer, reminded the audience. Leonard Dickinson, the GOP candidate for lieutenant governor, called Freeman and Humphrey "socialist sharpshooters," reminding voters that Eisenhower, commander of allied forces in Europe in World War II, "kept us out of war."[33]

Adlai Stevenson, the Democratic presidential candidate, visited Minneapolis on Saturday, September 29. Orville Freeman greeted him upon returning from a swing through the Red River Valley. There he had spoken on rural development at a meeting called to organize a regional economic-development corporation meant to invest in processing agricultural products.[34]

On the next day the *Sunday Tribune* offered welcome news to both candidates. The Minnesota Poll reported that Stevenson had cut Eisenhower's lead to a 49-to-47 percent margin. Freeman held a 51-to-42 percent lead over Nelsen. The Freeman-Nelsen race was tightening, however. Nelsen had cut Freeman's lead from a 19 percent spread in the June Minnesota Poll to a 9 percent spread in September.

The AFL and CIO held a historic meeting in Rochester the following week, where 1,400 delegates representing 200,000 union members voted to merge into a single union. Freeman was invited to speak, and the delegates "cheered to the rafters." Nelsen showed up uninvited. He asked to speak but "was received coldly" by the delegates.[35] The event offered a revealing contrast of the differing perspectives within the *Tribune* staff. Labor reporter Sam Romer covered the historic merger, detailing the delegates' enthusiasm for Freeman. Four days later the *Tribune* editorial writer mused, "It seems to us that Ancher Nelsen gained in stature with the general public, if not organized labor, by the boorish brush-off. Nelsen won the honors at Rochester for his courage and persistence, even if he didn't win many votes."[36]

The pace of the campaign as well as the press coverage started to pick up in early October. Nelsen attacked the civil-service plank in the

DFL platform, while Freeman challenged Nelsen to defend the GOP's farm program, linking the GOP candidate to flexible farm-price supports that declined along with farm prices. "Nelsen has yet to make a constructive suggestion on the farm situation," Freeman charged.[37] Nelsen and Leonard Dickenson criticized Freeman for taking credit for GOP accomplishments in the legislature and for making wild promises. The next day Freeman said, "The DFL stands on its record" while campaigning to good crowds in southern Minnesota.[38]

Four days later Nelsen picked up on Freeman's challenge on farm policy by supporting flexible farm-price supports and asking Freeman what he had done for farmers.[39] The next day Freeman chided the "Republican split personality," contrasting Nelsen's position with the endorsement of GOP Sen. Ed Thye and other major GOP leaders for rigid price supports. Two days later, on October 9, Freeman and Nelsen showed up for one of their few joint appearances, before the Minnesota Citizen Committee on Public Education. Both candidates supported the shift of iron-ore-tax funds from payment into trust funds to current education spending as well as an ease of restrictions in state borrowing from trust funds. Freeman proposed increased federal aid to education with Congress providing 50 percent of costs, while Nelsen limited federal assistance to 43 percent. Nelsen opposed withholding, describing the tax-collection method as a "temporary measure that takes in three years of tax payments in two years." Freeman supported pay-as-you-go withholding, suggesting the issue was forgiveness, the "exact amount of which has to be worked out."[40]

Two days later, Freeman returned to Carleton College in Northfield, where two years earlier a student rally had restored in him a sense of political confidence. A standing-room-only crowd of more than a thousand students and faculty members cheered as he detailed the differences between the DFL and GOP. The Carleton stop was the beginning of an extended tour taking Freeman south to the Iowa border and west to Austin, through Farmington and other communities. The reporter cited large crowds along main streets and at factory gates, where Freeman received "hearty receptions from working men and women."[41]

Freeman was working the basic strategy that had brought him victory in 1954. He pounded away on the losses to southern Minnesota, the heart of GOP voting strength, resulting from the Republican farm program. In 1954 diminished Republican margins had rewarded his efforts there. His objective was the same in the Sixth Congressional District; there Freeman reminded small-town merchants of their dependence on farm prosperity. He also cited the achievements of his first administration, describing them as a record the Republicans could not attack.[42] The Gallup Poll in late October confirmed the political judgment of Freeman's emphasis on southern Minnesota counties and other regions of GOP strength—the GOP was losing strength in the farm belt. Republican support was down 15 points from 1952, from 72 percent to 57 percent.[43] The Minnesota Poll predicted on Sunday, November 4, that Freeman would win with 52 percent of the vote, 48 percent for Nelsen.[44] The *Minneapolis Sunday Tribune*, however, refused to endorse either candidate, concluding that "generally Freeman has been a good governor [with] the vision to realize the importance of attracting new industry to Minnesota. Regardless of which one is elected, the state will have a better than average governor.[45]

If Stevenson had any chance in 1956 to defeat Eisenhower, international developments intervened to dash the hopes of the Democratic candidate. The Soviet Union invaded Hungary on October 30, toppling a government that had become too independent of Soviet authority. A day later, the British and French governments invaded Egypt, ousting President Gamel Nasser and reversing his nationalization of the Suez Canal. Eisenhower could not compel the Soviet Union to back away from Hungary, but he intervened to good effect in the Suez affair. The English and French backed down from the invasion, giving Nasser heroic status.[46] The American people, reminded four days before elections that the world was a scary place, now had the choice of staying with Eisenhower or going with Stevenson, a man with no experience in global politics. A Gallup Poll on November 13 found that the world crisis had shifted the vote to Eisenhower. The shift did not carry over to GOP candidates for the U.S. House and Senate.

Election Day in Minnesota

Freeman received 731,180 votes in the 1956 election while Ancher Nelsen, his opponent, received 685,196. Freeman won with a vote plurality of 45,984, a 51.8 percent margin—smaller than with his defeat of C. Elmer Anderson two years earlier. Early voting reports had predicted Freeman, cutting Republican margins in GOP counties in southern Minnesota, would end up outpolling Eisenhower.[47]

The victory was resounding nonetheless. Freeman polled 11,878 more votes than Eisenhower, a highly popular president who carried Minnesota by a 101,777-vote margin over Adlai Stevenson. The DFL remained in control of the Minnesota congressional delegation. Five DFL incumbents triumphed in a presidential election year, evidence of the organizational strength of the party and of Freeman's capacity to lead a statewide party ticket.

The victory in 1956 is significant for a several reasons. The DFL turned back a determined Republican challenge to cement its position as the dominant political party in Minnesota, confirming that the GOP would not easily reverse the 1954 shift in voting preferences in the state. Nelsen was not a political lightweight. He had won election as lieutenant governor in 1952. His choices politically were to preside over the Minnesota Senate for the next six years, assuming Anderson would win in 1954 and run again in 1956, or to find greener pastures in the Eisenhower administration. Soon after his election, he had re-signed to become head of the Rural Electrical Administration (REA).

After his defeat in 1956, Nelsen became chair of the Minnesota GOP. Again his stay was brief. He returned to Washington in 1958, elected by the voters of Minnesota's Second District to the U.S. House of Representatives.

The vulnerability of Republicans in Minnesota was evident. No GOP candidate was left standing in 1956 to carry the GOP ticket for statewide offices in 1958. This left Sen. Ed Thye to head the GOP ticket. Thye, a pleasant, kindly politician, had served one term as governor in 1944 before running for the U.S. Senate in 1946, when the GOP swept national elections to gain a two-year majority in the U.S. House. But the Republicans were unable to overcome the margin of Democratic control in the U.S. Senate. Thye's political fortunes held again in 1952, when he won reelection skidding on the Eisenhower landslide. The lack of a GOP tide in 1958, however, left the state party a spent force, unable to counter the rising political enthusiasm within the DFL.

Freeman emerged as the popular head of a vibrant new political party. The commitment of a decade of his and his family's lives to public service at last had borne The Minnesota Labor's League for Political Action political fruit. Stepping from under Hubert H. Humphrey's political shadow, Freeman had demonstrated his competence as a strong, independent leader. The two friends, in less than a decade, had together changed the face of Minnesota politics. With almost no money, Freeman had fashioned from dedicated activists a newly disciplined political party through new techniques of political organizing energized by innovations in communication technology. Each campaign proved a testing ground for the next. With Freeman's fine-tuning of the DFL campaign organization, the 1958 campaign would prove his best by far.

Sniffing the political winds for the coming legislative session, the Minnesota Poll reported that 60 percent of Minnesotans supported tax withholding. "It's easier to pay taxes [that way]," one respondent said. Another countered that withholding "is a burden on the employer." These polls were more accurate than the projections of the U.S. Department of Agriculture (USDA). One USDA official told North Dakota farmers in Devils Lake that the Eisenhower administration expected farm programs to trim price-depressing grain surpluses within three years.[48] Elsewhere, the department called for increased farm production, starting in 1960, when present surpluses would be exhausted.[49] A Gallup Poll five days later confirmed that GOP support among farmers dropped to 54 percent in 1956, a loss of 13 percent since 1952.[50]

*Chief Justice Roger Dell swore in Gov. Orville L. Freeman
on Janurary 7, 1959, after his winning 1958 campaign.*

—4—

The 1958 Campaign

G ov. Orville L. Freeman faced an embarrassment of political riches in the summer of 1957, a dilemma he would not have thought possible four years earlier. His loss in the 1952 campaign for governor had left him drifting emotionally and politically. His enemies had dismissed him as a political leader, while few of his political friends strongly disagreed. Indeed, neither did Freeman himself. But now he was on an emotional high, asking himself the question that every astute political observer discussed: Would he run in 1958 for a third term as governor or campaign for Minnesota's second U.S. Senate seat? Republican incumbent Edward J. Thye, a pleasant but ineffectual GOP leader, held the seat going into the 1958 race.

Successive Minnesota Polls found that the state's voters gave Governor Freeman an approval rating consistently at the high end of 60 percent. His peers considered him the dominant political figure in Minnesota government. He felt confident he could win either race. Freeman believed the Democratic-Farmer-Labor endorsement for the Senate race was his for the asking, a view few observers would challenge.

Though he later asked party leaders quietly for their advice, the success of the 1957 legislative session ending May 5 boosted his confidence. The political rhythms distinguishing DFL from Republican policy objectives that had emerged in the 1955 legislative session were now set. Freeman believed a governor is elected to lead. As governor and DFL leader, he challenged the legislature and Minnesota voters to look to the future. He treated each biennial legislative session as a time to examine how the government could prepare the state and its citizens to do that. Steps taken now to elevate the creative interaction of individual citizens, communities, labor, industry, and the economy would provide well-paying jobs, better services, sound education for all students, and a sustainable environment.

In 1957 Freeman proposed an increase in spending for education, health, and welfare services, together with programs to rebuild and expand the infrastructure of state government. He submitted a 17 percent increase in spending but asked for no increase in tax rates. He proposed a 6 percent increase in per-pupil state aid to schools, $200 per-pupil assistance to junior colleges, a $5 million revolving fund for construction aid to hard-pressed public schools, a loan program to assist the building of community nursing homes, a pay increase for state employees and state university faculty and staff, and a million-dollar grant to begin developing the seaport of Duluth in anticipation of the opening of the St. Lawrence Seaway in 1958.

But Freeman also asked the legislature to modernize Minnesota's tax structure according to the recommendations of the Governor's Tax Study Committee he had appointed earlier. The study, initiated in 1955 by a committee of Minnesota citizens and chaired by Minneapolis banker J. Cameron Thomson, proposed revamping the state tax structure from top to bottom. Its goal was to develop a tax climate friendlier to business and industry, by providing greater equity between and among taxpayers, a fairer tax system for individuals, improved enforcement, and withholding (pay-as-you-go) as a means to minimize tax cheaters and end the one-time lump-sum payment that burdened wage-earners. While Freeman had proposed withholding in 1955, the committee provided nonpartisan argument in 1957 that withholding was part of a fair, progressive tax system.

Freeman asked for party designation of state legislators to improve government accountability. He said the legislature should reorganize state government to improve the efficiency and effectiveness of the executive branch. He proposed a bonus for Minnesota veterans of the Korean War—to be paid from the windfall provided by taxes paid on previous and current years during the first year of withholding. He said half the revenue windfall would cover the cost.

The legislative session demonstrated the central role of the political party in Freeman's approach to public policy. Returning World War II veterans joined with the recently enfranchised women voters of Minnesota to infuse new political energy into state politics. But building public support and organizing the political power that could turn good intentions into programs and services required the continuity and political clout of a strong institutional base. The growth of non-government organizations (NGO) such as the educational, mental-health, and higher-education groups emerging to influence public policy could provide some but not all of that base.

An institution is an entity capable of planning and organizing and of providing its own memory. DFL members were idealists, and all but a few were volunteers, most with a decidedly pragmatic streak. The DFL was to support an active role for government in social and economic policy, to open new channels encouraging citizen participation in shaping policy, and to establish a lasting commitment to public accountability. The DFL offered no opportunity for patronage while out of power and none while in power. The merit system provides for almost all of the jobs in Minnesota government. The few governor-appointed positions carried qualifications rigorous enough to make them of little value as political prizes.

The DFL became both the catalyst for a new form of democratic governance in Minnesota and the glue holding together a political structure supporting liberal policies. Election was necessary to obtain the political authority to create legal foundations for new policies—the rule of law. Public office was a platform for explaining new policies to the public while informing DFL members and supporters of the work ahead. The DFL and its extensive use of government advisory committees and citizen councils were vehicles for citizen participation. And party designation enabled citizens to punish or reward the political party—the nongovernment institution responsible and accountable for public policy.

Freeman's actions as governor reflected his commitment to the DFL less as a vehicle for personal ambition and more as an institution for advancing the broad public interest. An examination of the critical decisions of his governorship as to whether they strengthened the party or the person reveals that he enhanced the party as a political institution every time. In the 1957 legislative session, Freeman recognized the advantage of incumbency in linking a DFL agenda to government activities. Simultaneously, since the Republicans did little to present a distinctive set of political alternatives, he implicitly called Republican values into question. The GOP limited its political goals in 1957 to supporting party designation and reapportionment and proposed a state convention to draft a new Minnesota constitution.[1]

Republican coherence on policy was apparent mainly in its opposition to Freeman's reform agenda. The DFL majority in the House through January and February 1957 considered the governor's reform program in committee hearings, approving in early April an omnibus tax bill and legislation to reorganize state government. In mid-April near the end of the 90-day legislative session, the Senate, led by a Conservative majority, struck down withholding in the Senate tax committee, effectively ending prospects for tax reform in 1957.[2]

J. Cameron Thomson, chair of the tax-study committee, had no comment, while Donald C. Dayton, one of seven members representing the business community on the 20-person committee, said he was "most disappointed." David Lilly, president of Toro Manufacturing and a vice chair of the study committee, said it was "too much to expect the adoption of a complex plan in a single session." He obliquely blamed Freeman for the loss, noting that it was "unfortunate that no bill embodying all the specific recommendations was offered to the legislature."[3]

Sen. Don Fraser (DFL-Minneapolis), a member of the Senate tax committee, said, "It is too bad that we couldn't give a little less partisan and a more careful consideration to the good proposal."[4] The Conservative majority rejected his amendment to forgive half of the income tax obligation for 1958.

Fraser pinpointed a weakness in Senate procedures having as much to do with the defeat of withholding as the exercise in partisanship. He offered an amendment on the Senate floor to override the committee bill to kill withholding. Senate Conservatives attacked Fraser's proposal as not germane—that is, the full Senate could not vote on it. Lt. Gov. Karl Rolvaag, a DFLer who also served as president of the Senate, ruled that Fraser's motion *was* germane. The Conservative majority then voted to overrule Rolvaag. "We might as well throw out the committee system" as reject a committee report, the Conservatives argued.[5]

The Conservatives were skilled procedural tacticians when it came to defeating DFL initiatives. The Senate defeated party designation first by amending the bill in committee to extend the designation to officials of local government, and then by voting down the legislation in the Senate to "save" local officials from party designation.[6] Two weeks later, when the legislature refused to change membership on the Railroad and Warehouse Commission from an elected to an appointed position (thus allowing the commissioners to continue as elected officials), the bill for government reorganization died.[7]

Measuring by the success of legislative reforms looking beyond the biennium, one might consider the 1957 legislative session a failure. But with no fiscal or other crisis focusing its attention, the legislature happily addressed meat-and-potato issues. It increased funding for current programs—schools, health and welfare, labor benefits, higher education, state employee salaries, and building programs.

The legislature approved a $398-million spending package in May for the 1958–59 biennium, some $15 million more than Freeman had requested in January and $72 million more than was approved for 1956–57. It authorized a $56-million state building program, about a million less than Freeman had requested but at twice the level approved in the previous biennium. The legislature authorized spending $236 million for education programs, about $17 million more than Freeman had requested and $52 million more than for 1956–57.

And, while raising state spending, the legislature repealed a five-dollar per taxpayer "head tax" favored by the Conservatives and slightly lowered the personal-property levy. Even without the withholding windfall, it also approved a pared-down bonus for Korean War veterans. It increased workmen's compensation benefits and approved a state college system to replace state teachers' colleges with an increase in faculty salaries. It approved measures raising per-pupil state aid from $82 to $85. It increased old-age benefits, and ever mindful of public health conservation, the legislature banned piranhas, a tropical fish, from Minnesota rivers and lakes.[8]

While the *Minneapolis Sunday Tribune* tallied the accomplishments of the 1957 session on page 1, J. Cameron Thomson lamented on the business page that the "area is not able to provide jobs for its surplus population, particularly young people. We need a growing, diversified economy." The chair of the Minnesota Governor's Tax Committee did not mention tax reform.[9]

Given the positive outcome of the session, Freeman labeled the results a "constructive and forward-looking accomplishment."[10] He said the absence of tax reform and government reorganization was disappointing, but he did not dwell on either. After two sessions, the DFL had demonstrated its ability to govern Minnesota effectively. It could claim to represent the views of a majority of voters.

Freeman recognized that the 1958 election would nail down the DFL mantle of political leadership as well as his own. The election loomed large in the minds of DFL leaders at the end of the 1957 legislative session. Freeman began canvassing those he trusted among the party leadership. Eugenie Anderson, a Red Wing resident and long-time party activist, did not hide her interest in running for the nomination herself. Lt. Gov. Karl Rolvaag, who also harbored senatorial ambitions, urged Freeman to run for a third term, arguing that as the head of the ticket his strength would carry other candidates. Ray Hemenway, state DFL chair, strongly endorsed a third term. Gerald Heaney, as close to Freeman as any advisor and by this time Minnesota's national Democratic committeeman, was emphatic: Freeman should use his political strength to keep the DFL in control of state government while electing a DFL candidate to the U.S. Senate. With Freeman as head of the ticket, Heaney viewed the 1958 race as an opportunity to increase the Democratic majority in the U.S. Senate just before the 1960 presidential election. Oddly, Hubert Humphrey was ambivalent.[11]

The decision was Freeman's, and he chose to run for a third term in 1958. An executive by temperament, Freeman knew he could not sit easily fashioning compromises as a legislator.[12] More important, Freeman believed his task was "building the DFL Party. That was the work I set out in 1948 to do after Humphrey was elected to the Senate, and the job was not yet finished. Public confidence in the DFL had been restored, but the rebuilding of Minnesota state government was unfinished and required a strong DFL Party."[13]

Selecting the Senate Candidate

The last piece of unfinished business in organizing the 1958 campaign was selection of the Senate candidate. The process began with a meeting of the DFL executive committee in January to discuss the qualifications guiding its search for potential candidates. The primary qualification must be political leadership, with ability to win and hold elective office a basic principle, the executive committee concluded.

"First crack should be given to DFL members of Congress," Democratic national committeeman Heaney observed.[14] Like others, he was aware that Freeman, who did not participate in the discussions, had taken himself out of contention and would strongly support Eugenie Anderson.

One by one, the executive committee reviewed the five DFL members of Congress. John Blatnik, Seventh District, had won reelection handily in 1956. But his opponent had charged that Blatnik was a Communist 20 years earlier; the congressman did not relish the rough-and-tumble of a campaign that would revisit the issue statewide. Roy Wier, in the Third District, would have strong labor support from his Minneapolis base, but he took no interest in campaigning statewide. Coya Knutson was embroiled in an ugly family feud embellished by an intense split of the DFL organization in the Ninth District; she was unlikely to receive endorsement for reelection by the DFL district convention. Fred Marshall was highly popular in the Sixth District but wanted to stay in the House. All but one person agreed that Rep. Eugene McCarthy, in the Fourth District, was similarly content.

"Someone should talk to Gene," Heaney said. "He should be asked. We need to know for sure." Other committee members took no interest in following up Heaney's suggestion, even though those from the Twin Cities were the logical contacts. The committee left the issue with Heaney, who lived in Duluth. In the meantime, other members of the executive committee moved quickly to Eugenie

Anderson, the first woman appointed ambassador to Denmark and a DFL leader with strong support among the party's women.

Heaney approached McCarthy soon thereafter. "Are you interested in running for the Senate seat?" he asked. "Has anyone in the party discussed this with you?"

"Yes." McCarthy said he wanted the nomination and intended to run. "No," he answered the second question. No other among the party leadership had discussed the Senate race with him.

By the time Heaney could report his conversation with McCarthy to the other members of the executive committee, Anderson's campaign already had begun. Many if not most members of the executive committee supported her candidacy. The opportunity to head off a bruising confrontation, if ever possible, was gone. Now the founders of the DFL were choosing up sides.

Taking an early start, McCarthy announced his candidacy February 1. Labor, one of the old Farmer-Labor twins, supported him strongly. The old Democratic Party, largely the home of Catholic voters in Minnesota and centered in St. Paul, was firmly in his camp as well. In effect, two factions of the tripartite DFL structure, both with a strong base for funding and organizing members in DFL strongholds, were campaigning early and energetically for the DFL endorsement for McCarthy. But Anderson also had a healthy base of support. Women, a postwar pillar of the DFL, as well as urban, liberal, party members, were energetically organizing to elect Anderson delegates to the state DFL convention. Anderson, however, did not announce her bid for the Senate nomination until April 12. She did so at a dinner in Red Wing, where the absence of top party leaders was noticeable but not mentioned in news reports. The top representative of the Freeman administration was Arthur Naftalin, commissioner of administration, her lead speaker.[15]

As the delegates to the state convention assembled in Rochester in June, the McCarthy forces were tantalizingly close to securing the nomination. Under party rules at the time, a two-thirds vote of the convention was necessary for endorsement. McCarthy's forces believed they could count on 62 percent of delegate support at the peak of their voting strength. They could not secure the nomination outright.

In one of the great ironies of Minnesota political history, a woman gave McCarthy the margin to secure nomination and sure victory in securing the state's second DFL U.S. Senate seat. Coya Knutson had come to Rochester without the endorsement of the Ninth District convention for her reelection. She was the first and only woman elected to Congress in Minnesota during the 20th century. She had served two terms representing a district covering the northwest corner of the state. The Ninth District DFL was split in a personal feud between Knutson's supporters and opponents. That, in addition to publication of the famous "Coya, come home" letter, supposedly written by her husband, was politically devastating. The true author, subsequently identified in congressional hearings, was L. J. Lee, chair of the Ninth District DFL.

Under party rules, the state DFL convention could endorse congressional candidates even where a district convention failed to agree on a nominee. Knutson's supporters controlled about 5 percent of the delegates to the state convention, a bloc sufficient to give senatorial endorsement to McCarthy. As Heaney recounts, the McCarthy campaign agreed to swing its support behind Knutson's endorsement for reelection in the Ninth District. In return, Knutson's supporters provided McCarthy with the margin needed to gain endorsement by the DFL for his candidacy for the U.S. Senate.[16]

Although the McCarthy forces had the votes for endorsement, the Coya bloc held back on the first ballot. On the second, McCarthy easily won the contest. Anderson conceded the nomination and moved that the convention choose McCarthy by acclamation. Thus the 1958 DFL state convention decided the political fate of both women.

The opportunity of the DFL to elect the first Minnesota woman to the U.S. Senate was gone. Freeman was at the peak of his political strength as governor; the DFL was stronger and more united than ever before or since.[17] Furthermore, the 1958 campaign represented the culmination of Freeman's mastery of political organizing, during which the DFL emerged as a disciplined, tightly coordinated political entity like none seen before in Minnesota. Barring any lapse of judgment or error, the 1958 DFL candidate for the U.S. Senate was as close to a sure bet for election as could occur in Minnesota. The 1958 DFL convention in Rochester nominated Freeman for reelection and selected Eugene McCarthy to head the ticket with him. It endorsed Representative Knutson, as were all other incumbent congressional candidates for reelection. It endorsed Joseph Karth, a state representative and a labor official, as the DFL candidate for McCarthy's Fourth District seat in the House.

The Campaign

The 1958 campaign represents the culmination of Freeman's technique, innovation, and organizational skills, which fueled the DFL's swift rise to political dominance in Minnesota. In the 1954 campaign, Freeman exploited television to establish a new political identity for the DFL and hammered out a political framework that gained the support of a majority of Minnesota voters. The involvement of volunteers in organizing and running the campaign, initially a necessity for the underfunded political party, became an identifying characteristic. The introduction of the sample ballot carried a unique message for the time: The candidates ran as a political team that voters could elect and hold accountable.

In 1956, the DFL sharpened and refined the techniques it had introduced in 1954. All state office candidates operated from one campaign headquarters at one location so that campaign staff could communicate and coordinate activities. Each candidate, for the most part, stayed on the same message. The chair of the DFL Party and Freeman's campaign manager operated as a team. Freeman's managerial skills, first evident in the intense overhaul of state budget recommendations in 1955, now reshaped the organization of state campaigns. By 1958, the party leaders had analyzed each element of the previous campaign, identified changes that could improve performance, and introduced a timeline planning the campaign from election day back to the start of the campaign. The concept enabled the coordination of fundraising with the planning of expenditures for advertising and campaign activities, provided potential contributors with hard evidence of where there was need and how funds would be used, and allowed the campaign manager to coordinate staff and volunteer responsibilities with campaign events.

In 1958 Freeman found a campaign manager who was as tough and hard-driving as he. Walter F. Mondale had gone to school on managing statewide political campaigning under Freeman. He was every bit as intense and demanding. Mondale had become a party activist in 1946 as a freshman at Macalester College in St. Paul, where he organized the Second District for Humphrey's 1948 campaign for the U.S. Senate even before he could vote. Drafted for service in the Korean War in 1951, he returned to finish law school at the University of Minnesota in 1954. Mondale coordinated suburban campaign activities in the Twin Cities when the DFL emerged on center stage in 1954. And he was deputy campaign manager with responsibilities for planning and coordinating campaigning in Minnesota's nine congressional districts in 1956. His analyses and reports for the 1956 campaign demonstrate a keen political instinct for organization and management, as well as the conflict and attraction between two Alpha-type personalities.

"Freeman's political genius was his ability to recognize and enlist individuals with unique skills and abilities into politics," a longtime DFL participant observed.[18] Regardless of personal conflicts, Freeman had watched and appreciated Mondale's organizing ability as it had developed over the past decade. Freeman wanted, and got, the best person for the job.[19] For his part, Mondale welcomed the opportunity to demonstrate his managerial and organizational skills.

The emergence of the DFL and Freeman's role in shaping the party as a cohesive, well-organized political institution, was gaining recognition in national political circles. Foster Furcolo, then governor of Massachusetts, wrote Freeman on July 21, 1958, for advice on campaign techniques for letting voters know of the Furcolo administration's accomplishments. Freeman's reply a month later is a meticulous outline in planning voter-education programs. In a backhand slap at past Republican governors, it also reveals his dislike of political cynicism.

Freeman and his staff believed that his GOP predecessors had practiced political sleight-of-hand with voters. Republican governors often publicly lavished attention on one highly popular program, such as mental health, to impress the voters. They treated other programs and services, however, with benign neglect. Freeman's shock upon examining the state budget as he and his advisors rewrote spending proposals for the 1955 legislative session only confirmed his belief that his predecessors had practiced a casual approach to the public's business.

"One of the frustrations of having an administration [that] works in every area of state government is that you do not become identified with one or two very popular issues alone," Freeman wrote Governor Furcolo.[20] Further:

> In our radio, television, and newspaper advertising beamed at the general electorate, it is not feasible to itemize in detail the accomplishments in each area. We, therefore, take one area at a time and tie it into the general campaign theme of "Keep a Working Government." In order to achieve recognition in each of the areas of government, we have set up special com-

mittees in several areas: Independents, Veterans, Farmers, Welfare, Conservation, Education, Business Development, Labor, Civil Rights, and so on.

Each of these committees considers, generally, activities using the following techniques: Mailing memos or letter to their special-interest groups after obtaining the necessary mailing lists, advertising in special-interest journals, radio and television spots and programs, press releases, and appearances by myself and others.

Freeman's letter to Furcolo describes a political leader with an executive command of organizational detail. His campaign staff was in charge of the issue-sectors committees, the congressional-district tours, and most of the fundraising.[21] The DFL and its chair were responsible for planning and organizing voter-registration drives, statewide distribution of campaign literature, preparation and mailing of sample ballots with endorsed DFL candidates, and financing and organizing of statewide television and radio programs. In practice, Freeman's campaign manager and the DFL chair jointly managed campaign operations, reporting regularly to Freemen through Tom Hughes, his executive assistant or secretary. Attached to the Furcolo letter were six detailed campaign documents, including an exhaustive analysis of the record of his Republican opponent in 1958, George E. MacKinnon.

Mondale went Freeman one better in preparing a detailed "order of battle" for the 1958 campaign. The attention to detail probably was intended as much to keep the governor at arm's length in managing the campaign as to ensure Mondale's control of campaign details.[22] Freeman was less likely to micromanage when he was confident every detail was being anticipated, every option weighed.

Mondale laid forth seven principles paramount in organizing and managing an effective campaign:

1. A closely and carefully planned backward-phased campaign program must be designed early in the campaign, prepared in readily usable form, outlining in substantial detail the projects to be undertaken, the time schedule, and the budget allocation. "This plan was of infinite value in the timing and planning of staff work, but it was also of value in the area of fundraising," Mondale wrote. "It went far to create confidence in the campaign and its management so that people felt their campaign contribution would be efficiently and effectively used."

2. A campaign headquarters and the campaign equipment should be of the highest standard. The location should be selected to ensure the staff will not be subjected to substantial interruption from visiting persons. The headquarters should be opened by the middle of June or the first of July.

3. Nothing is more critical to the conduct of a campaign than finding able staff members. There should be a full-time person in charge of office management, another in charge of outstate touring and special projects, and there should be at least one full-time writer, with at least one in reserve for the peak writing periods. There should be a full-time radio-and-television-production man and one secretary, preferably two. There should be a first-class advertising agency that is capable of competent technical work, and the same goes for an accountant. Staff should be paid whatever is necessary to demand of them a first-class, efficient, and timely job. We should obtain and pay whatever is necessary for people who can with creativity and re-sourcefulness handle their own areas in the campaign.[23]

4. The media campaign should be planned to do a few projects exceedingly well rather than attempt to undertake several scattered projects. A well-planned, carefully prepared campaign kickoff is one of the fine points in the campaign. A substantial amount of time should be put into the writing and staging of

the affair, adding to its professional stature and improving its effectiveness.

Similarly, concentration on planning and preparation of outstate tours, including substantial expenditures, brings commendable results. Preparation involves advance advertising of tours and purchase of districtwide radio and television advertising when the candidate is in the district.

5. A well-planned counterattack on the opposing candidate is important for an incumbent. In effect, ignoring the charges of an opponent gives the opposing candidate free spot announcements and advertising, since the attacks are the only political material arriving at media outlets. A drumfire of counterattack statements can be leveled by all other candidates sharing the party ticket. Statements should be hand-delivered to the staff of television stations and newspapers, insisting they be used along with the opposition's charges. Television stations will tend to drop the charges entirely, or give them insignificant play, while newspapers will relegate all charges to news graveyards, i.e., "Political Notes."

6. Registration and voter drives should be given the highest priority. Canvassing in heavily DFL voting areas should be done before and after registration closes and on election day in conjunction with phone banks for getting out the vote. The DFL should consider establishing a permanent registration and election-day get-out-the-vote office jointly financed by all liberal organizations.

7. Coordination of the campaigns of the various candidates is essential. Central location of campaign headquarters will ensure higher campaign coordination than otherwise possible and influence every facet of a campaign. A central campaign location is more efficient, economical, and has far more campaign impact. A central location also impresses the media.

In addition to the seven elements of campaign organization, Mondale devoted considerable attention to budgeting. He recommended breaking the campaign budget into two categories—the first detailing essential campaign expenses such as staff, space, and equipment; the second identifying proposed expenditures in campaigning, including radio, television, travel, and others. The second category was based primarily on a media chart, also listing the basic policy decisions that formed campaign parameters.

To accompany the two-phase expenditure budget, Mondale projected anticipated income, listing major sources of contributions and other revenues according to estimates of minimum and maximum receipts likely from each source. As the campaign progressed, Mondale received a weekly report of contributions and expenditures. With this and a weekly report on purchases based on a system of purchase-order records, he could develop a weekly running total and show the financial status of the campaign.

Things in the Republican camp were not going as smoothly for Ancher Nelsen, whom Freeman defeated in the 1956 campaign for governor but who now served as chair of the Minnesota GOP.[24] He had trouble finding an opponent for Freeman in 1958. In April, as Anderson and McCarthy maneuvered for the DFL Senate nomination, Harold LeVander, a leading GOP figure, said, "I will not be a candidate for governor in 1958."[25]

Nelsen lamented dolefully: "I regret he won't be in the contest. I hope others step up and indicate their interest. I would like to know if M. Wayne Field or George MacKinnon will permit their names to be considered in the Republican primaries." Field was the aggressive 34-year-old head of the Hope Chest Company, a fast-growing Golden Valley business. Appointed U.S. attorney for Minnesota by President Eisenhower, MacKinnon had represented the Third District for one term (1947–49) in Congress and served for three terms in the Minnesota House of Representatives (1935–41). MacKinnon said he hoped the GOP would get someone else to run, but he was "giving serious consideration" to the idea.[26]

Field formally opened his campaign for governor two days later. Announcing his candidacy in Mankato, the former head of the Minnesota Junior Chamber of Commerce proposed adoption of a Minnesota sales tax. He supported the Eisenhower program advocated by Secretary of Agriculture Ezra Taft Benson to lower farm-price supports, and he endorsed a right-to-work law for Minnesota.[27]

Faced in June with the choice of a Republican who was reluctant to run and a candidate who bluntly stated Republican positions, the Republican state convention in Minneapolis endorsed George E. MacKinnon for governor.[28]

Minnesotans in general probably were not giving politics much attention in the spring and early summer of 1958. Forest fires raged through northern Minnesota. Judy Garland, born Francis Gumm in Grand Rapids, had agreed to sing for her supper at a Minnesota Centennial gala. The celebration had started in Winona (the first community to learn of Minnesota's statehood in 1858) with a special nine-car train containing 115 exhibits that would visit 97 communities over the next eight months.[29] This was also the year that the United States dropped World War II treason charges against Ezra Pound and the Eisenhower administration called on France to end the Algerian War.

Unemployment continued to rise, however, and Freeman sought to offset any unrest among voters. He directed state agencies to accelerate construction and other building projects, and he urged city and county governments to take similar action. Freeman also called on U.S. Steel (USS), the parent company of Oliver Mining Company, to build a taconite plant in Minnesota. He noted that the company had shipped 1.3 billion tons of iron ore and asked company executives to meet with him to discuss plans. A month later Roger Blough, head of USS, with Freeman at his side, said the company would open a taconite plant within a decade. The decision rested on tax assistance, he said. Freeman promised the preferential tax rates on taconite would continue.[30]

Freeman benefited from current events other than those furthered by his own political instincts during the summer of 1958. The USDA reduced dairy price supports by 19 cents per hundredweight. The decision cost Minnesota dairy farmers $13 million in lost income but resulted in no increase in consumption as consumer prices remained low. MacKinnon mounted a relentless attack with increasingly shrill charges that sought to link Freeman with Minneapolis organized crime—this in an effort to drive up Freeman's negatives (the number of voters responding negatively to his name). The outcome in November seemed inevitable. The voters dismissed MacKinnon, who damaged Thye's hopes for reelection in the process.

The 1958 recession was hurting Minnesota, however, and the governor's office was worried. "Governor," Dorothy Jacobson said, repeating in mid-October a plea she had been making for several weeks, "you should tell people that taxes will need to be raised next year to maintain state services."[31] She had tracked economic data from state agencies during the past year. With unemployment-compensation cases up 36 percent in 1958 from the previous year, she knew revenues from personal income taxes would be down in 1959.[32] As Freeman's campaign for a third term drew to a close, she argued once again. "You should tell people before election day. Otherwise people will say you withheld the information until after you were reelected."

Two facts were common knowledge in October in the governor's office and elsewhere in Minnesota political circles: One, as the *Minneapolis Star* noted in endorsing Freeman, was that he "has a commanding lead" over his opponent, Republican George MacKinnon.[33] The *Star*'s editorial writer complained that Freeman was "avoiding discussion of issues that might threaten his lead," while dismissing MacKinnon for running a "smearing attack on Freeman." The other fact commonly known was the 1958 recession.[34] While brightening national election prospects for Democrats across the country, the economic slowdown also ensured that state governments would confront revenue shortfalls. Minnesota, like most other states, faced a deficit. The cost of state government in the 1960–61 biennium would outrun likely revenues even without adding new programs in the January 1959 legislative session. Estimates available in the governor's office in late September speculated that the deficit in the next biennium would exceed $70 million.

Freeman initially dismissed the issue.[35] The economy, he argued in his campaign statements, appeared to be recovering from the recession. He hoped any deficit might disappear before the next year. Other voices sang in favor of a tax message before election, however. University of Minnesota economics professor Walter Heller, an influential tax advisor, and Minnesota Tax Commissioner Joseph Robertson agreed with Jacobson. Freeman was upset that the reality of governing was becoming a specter just as he savored what was likely to be the greatest victory of his political career.

Like every politician (regardless of polls and his own sense of public support for his campaign), Freeman did not want to jeopardize his election. He would win, he knew. The question was—by how much? As head of the ticket, Freeman understood the opportunity his vote potential offered the DFL. He wanted a margin large enough to assure the election of Fouth District Congressman Eugene McCarthy as the first Catholic senator from the state.[36] He wanted to build the 16-vote DFL margin in the Minnesota House. He wanted to defeat the Conservative leadership in the Senate and elect a Liberal DFL majority.

The success of the DFL in the previous two state elections had encouraged strong DFL candidates to run for the state legislature in 1958. Gerry Dillon, head of a Minneapolis printing company and a key Freeman political advisor, was running against Donald O. Wright of Minneapolis. Wright, who had been elected to the state legislature in 1929 and who served as chair of the Senate tax committee, was

Freeman's longtime Conservative nemesis. Howard E. Smith, chair of the Crow Wing County DFL, was running against Gordon Rosenmeier, a Little Falls Conservative who chaired the Senate civil administration committee and blocked government reorganization. Freeman wanted a DFL sweep. He wanted it all.

Reluctantly, Freeman agreed to make a speech on taxes, asking Jacobson to prepare a draft. A week before election day, on October 28, Freeman delivered a half-hour radio address on "Financing the Services of State Government."[37] On the same day, the *Minneapolis Star,* while endorsing Freeman for reelection, declared, "We think the governor ought to have discussed the state's finances in more detail. His hope that the increased economic activity will yield additional revenues may not be realized. He still ought to give serious attention to the use of a sales tax."[38]

The tax speech received detailed coverage in the *Minneapolis Tribune* on October 29. Russell Hurst reported that Freeman supported withholding and opposed a sales tax. Hurst wrote that the governor would base his tax program for the 1959 legislative session on an income tax—that is on the ability to pay—and would stress fairness. A tax climate favorable to business was one major goal, as was obtaining revenues adequate to pay for public services.

Freeman said in his speech that he would raise "additional revenues that might be required" should tax receipts be insufficient in 1959. He said the state constitution required the governor to submit a balanced budget. He refrained from suggesting cuts in public services. He said he would follow the advice given two years earlier by the Minnesota Governor's Tax Study Committee. In his words:

The present tax structure should be continually strengthened and adjusted to keep it effective, equitable, and contributing to the economic progress of the state. We [Minnesotans] do not now, nor will we in the immediate future, face the possibility of adopting new taxes, providing we make full and intelligent use of our present tax system. Our principal reliance should continue to be on a true progressive personal income tax and a well-balanced corporate income tax, keeping in mind that a reasonable share of increased burdens should be assigned to the iron ore, gross earnings, selective excises, and other existing taxes.

The prospects for raising substantial additional revenues appear to lie principally in introduction of a sales or value-added tax, and in raising effective rates applicable under the individual income tax.

The *Tribune* editorialized the next day, October 30, that it was "disappointed the governor flatly opposed the general sales tax." Three days later the paper endorsed Freeman for reelection, noting that "we approve of much of what he said on financing state government."

MacKinnon, his campaign spiraling downward, used Freeman's tax message as the basis for a personal attack. Freeman is a "tax ignoramus [with] a lack of knowledge of basic rudiments of taxation," he said, ironically accusing the governor of avoiding a discussion of taxes.[39] He did not recognize Freeman's "additional revenues that might be required" as an opening to charge that he intended to raise taxes. Neither did he join the metropolitan press in criticizing Freeman for opposing a sales tax.

Governor Freeman won reelection on November 4 with a margin of 167,595 votes, helping to elect Rep. Eugene McCarthy to the U.S. Senate. McCarthy defeated Sen. Ed Thye by 73,213 votes. The DFL increased its Liberal majority by one seat in the Minnesota House and by six Liberal seats in the state Senate, leaving the Conservative caucus with a 40-vote margin. Wright barely survived Gerry Dillon's challenge with a seven-vote margin. Rosenmeier lost his home county of Crow Wing but defeated Gordon Smith by 2,800 votes.

Gov. Orville Freeman declared martial law to prevent violence at the Wilson and Company meatpacking plant in Albert Lea. National Guardsmen protected the entrance to the plant, above, on December 11, 1959.

—5—

Albert Lea & the Wilson Strike

A full-scale riot erupted shortly after 4 P.M. on December 9, 1959, at the Wilson and Company meatpacking plant in Albert Lea, Minnesota. About 400 nonunion workers, most hired by Wilson as strikebreakers during the preceding week, were leaving the plant as the shift changed. More than 700 members of the United Packinghouse Workers of America (UPWA), who had been on strike for five weeks, blocked the gate.

As the second shift of strikebreakers arrived, a strikebreaker gunned his car engine, knocking down a striker and injuring his head. Word passed swiftly: a strikebreaker with a rifle was threatening strikers. Tempers flared at the rumor, and the strikers moved to block all the plant gates. Rocks flew, and most of the strikebreakers retreated into the plant for safety. Car windows shattered. Flying glass hit a nonunion worker, blinding him in one eye. Three cars were overturned, another pushed into nearby Albert Lea Lake.

The din mounted. By 6 P.M. another 300 strikers joined the melee. Twenty Albert Lea policemen, the city's full force, came on the scene. Thirty Freeborn County sheriff's deputies joined them. With some

350 strikebreakers still inside and hoping to get past a thousand angry strikers, the police force had too little manpower to disperse them. It didn't try the hopeless task.

Police searched the vehicles of strikebreakers, confiscating three pistols, seven automatic rifles, two shotguns, and assorted knives. The search provided union leaders a lull to talk with the strikers. Using police bullhorns, they urged union members to proceed to their union hall a mile away for a special strike meeting. The crowd, eager for a way out of the evening's confrontation, slowly dispersed. By 7:30 the strikebreakers could leave safely.

The next morning, December 10, began quietly. But by early afternoon, the number of strikers crowding the picket line had grown. The wives of some workers joined the crowd, swelling to more than 700 strong by 4 P.M., another shift change. Massing some 50 officers and deputies, now better prepared to quell a riot, police officials kept the crowd under control—but only at a cost. The tension forced the city and the county to keep all available personnel at the plant, neglecting their peacekeeping duties elsewhere. Vandals threw bricks through the windows of grocery stores carrying Wilson meat products, but the police could not respond. Neither could deputies deter attacks on farms where strikebreakers lived.

City and county officials believed the community had reached its breaking point. Another confrontation, likely to come sooner rather than later, was inevitable. Gov. Orville L. Freeman had sent a two-man team to monitor the situation. Now Minnesota Highway Safety Director Harry Sieben and Minnesota Labor Conciliator Charles W. Johnson met with the officials of Albert Lea, a city of 12,000. Many of its citizens were UPWA members who had worked most of their lives in the Wilson plant, the community's major employer. Albert Lea had grown to encircle the plant, but Wilson and Company had kept its operations legally in the township, outside the city limits, to avoid paying city taxes. The township, a subcounty government that did little more than serve the Wilson plant, contracted with Albert Lea to provide police services there.

Local officials told Sieben and Johnson that the community needed time to calm down. Another riot was imminent. Fellow citizens had turned into strikers and strikebreakers. Friends and neighbors were fighting, and someone was likely to die by morning. The consequences of further violence might include personal hatred festering for decades. The officials needed outside help. They agreed they could not restore calm with the plant remaining open.

Sieben reached for the telephone, then dialed Tom Hughes, the governor's executive secretary, who served as coordinator during the crisis.[1] Sieben said Albert Lea was poised to explode. Local officials had agreed the plant should be closed to avoid bloodshed and allow time for tensions to subside. Hughes told Sieben to stand by—Freeman would call back shortly. Hughes then called the principal's office at Kandiyohi High School: "Please ask Governor Freeman to come to the phone." Freeman, who had been speaking at dedication ceremonies for the school's new gymnasium, listened quietly as Hughes gave him the message he expected but had hoped would never come.[2]

The governor immediately called Sieben, who reviewed the rising tensions around the Wilson plant, the sporadic violence, and vandalism. The city and county police force could not maintain order, Sieben said. The situation was spiraling out of control.

"What do you recommend?" Freeman asked. Sieben urged him to talk with the county attorney and city government officials about what actions might stabilize the situation before morning. Niles Shoff, the physician-elected-mayor of Albert Lea, came on the line, urging the governor to take charge. Freeborn County Sheriff Everett Sloan and Albert Lea Police Chief Charles Hellman repeated the plea. County Attorney Russell Olson told his old law-school classmate he feared for people's lives unless the state intervened. Freeman thanked them and said he would act swiftly to prevent further violence.

Hanging up the phone, the governor stood by the desk, alone, thinking. Reelected by the largest majority of his career, he was midway in his third term. He had wrapped his arms around Eugene McCarthy, ensuring the election of a Minnesota Catholic to the U.S. Senate. He had been campaigning through southwestern Minnesota to build support for the education, health, and social programs of the DFL. He had just concluded a bitter special session of the legislature to raise taxes to fund those programs. He knew his 1960 reelection contest would be tough and mean. The last thing he wanted to do as Christmas approached was respond to the crisis in Albert Lea. But every political leader faces unwelcome tasks, and his turn had come.

After his pause to think, Freeman moved swiftly. He called Hughes, a man of astute political judgment. Then he called Dorothy Jacobson, his policy advisor in the governor's office. He called his wife, Jane, to say it would be a busy night. Then he called on Miles Lord, the state's attorney general, to draft a martial-law decree for his signature. And he called Maj. Gen. Joseph E. Nelson, the state adjutant general and commander of the Minnesota National Guard.

"How much time do you need to put the guard in Albert Lea to close the Wilson plant?" Freeman asked.

Nelson answered, "Governor, you can't do that!"

"General, I didn't call you to get permission to close the plant. I asked you how long you need to get troops to Albert Lea, and I am ordering you to close the plant. I want you to have the troops there before the plant starts daily operations tomorrow morning," replied Freeman.[3] He asked Nelson to meet Miles Lord in the attorney general's office to help draw up the order proclaiming martial law. In his last call he informed Sieben and Johnson of his decision. He asked them to tell city and county officials of his intent to close the Wilson plant while limiting martial law to the township surrounding it.

The governor said farewell to the officials and citizens celebrating the dedication, without disclosing his decision, and climbed wearily into his limousine for the ride home. About 10 P.M. Attorney General Lord and General Nelson left their homes, to arrive at the capitol shortly before 11 P.M. Deputy Attorney General Robert Mattson joined them in the attorney general's office there.[4] Hughes waited for the martial-law decree at his desk in the governor's office across the hall, occasionally updating Sieben by phone.

The decree was ready for signature about 1:30 A.M.[5] With document in hand, Hughes drove on University Avenue toward Minneapolis, then across the Franklin Avenue bridge to Freeman's Seabury Avenue home. The governor arrived there from Kandiyohi about 2 A.M. Freeman scanned the decree order and signed it. Hughes drove back to the capitol and delivered the official order to Lord and Nelson, who immediately informed the lead elements of the National Guard awaiting orders to Albert Lea. At home, Freeman called his press secretary, Rod Leonard, around 3 A.M. to alert reporters to the governor's declaration of martial law and closing of the Wilson plant. Early morning radio and television news shows carried wire-service reports on the matter before the first troops arrived in Albert Lea.

About 4 A.M. on December 11, Maj. Gen. Richard Cook, commander of the 47th Infantry Division, drove up to the Wilson plant with a few officers—the vanguard of troops to follow. Four sleepy strikers on a symbolic picket line watched with surprise as the guard caravan stopped. Cook got out of the lead Jeep and announced the declaration of martial law. He ordered the strikers to disband. Surprised manager Clifford E. Cairns greeted him on his entry to the plant. Martial law had been declared, Cook said, and he was there to close the plant. Leo O'Neal, Wilson plant superintendent sleeping overnight in his office, emerged.

Cook said, "Leo, can I talk to you in your office?"[6] It was a command, not a request. The general told O'Neal the National Guard was taking over the plant. "I have a job to do. I don't like it any better than you do, but we have to do this."

93

Seething, O'Neal replied, "I guess you got the guns to do it."

Two hours later 90 troops from Company C of the 47th Division reached Albert Lea. Another 110 men from the Headquarters Company of the Second Battle Group, Mankato, arrived shortly afterward. Both units assumed positions at the Wilson plant at 6:30 A.M. to turn away the strikebreakers reporting for work. As the news spread through Albert Lea, UPWA members took to the plant. By 7 A.M., when General Cook read his plant closure order, the throng had grown to about 500. He ordered the troops—armed with rifles and fixed bayonets—to disband the crowd. The order met no resistance.

Closing a plant during a dispute between labor and management—even to restore community stability—simply was not done in the 1950s. Minnesota, however, had witnessed earlier conflicts between capital and labor that did not fit the conventional American pattern. Freeman did not realize at the time that he followed a tradition of innovative public policy by Minnesota governors responding to labor disputes. In his decision to protect citizens and the community interest, Freeman completed an evolution of labor-management policy that had begun at the turn of the century. With the perspective of time, the closing of the Wilson plant appears the logical outcome of social policy starting with John A. Johnson, the first 20th-century Democratic governor of Minnesota, and carried on by Floyd B. Olson, the first Farmer-Labor governor of the state. Freeman's action as the first DFL governor constituted a defining if informal commitment to workers by the DFL.

The earliest example of a Minnesota governor considering the role of the National Guard in an industrial dispute occurred in northern Minnesota as the 20th century began. Minnesota's Iron Range was the scene of tumultuous labor conflict and social unrest. Iron-ore miners were mostly unmarried because wages were so low they could not afford to raise families on the range. Mine owners claimed to pay two dollar a day, but after mandatory deductions for equipment, food, and other materials, the miners often received less than a dollar. Working conditions were intolerable; the workday averaged ten to 12 hours. Few men could endure the strain of the work for more than a year or two. Medical services for miners injured on the job did not exist, though the men had to pay a dollar a month for medical care.[7]

By 1905 the miners were organizing unions. Within two years, 14 unions across the range joined into a single organization affiliated with the Western Federation of Miners (WFM).[8] The mine owners, led by U.S. Steel Company, watched uneasily the growing unionism. They hired the Pinkerton Detective Company to spy on union members. Pinkerton identified leaders and prominent union members among the miners; then the companies fired the union leaders.

The WFM sent Oliver Mining Company, a U.S. Steel subsidiary, its list of demands on July 9, 1907, setting in motion a confrontation with U.S. Steel that eventually brought Governor Johnson into the conflict. The miners wanted an eight-hour workday and a minimum daily wage of $2.50 for miners working in open-surface pits. They wanted $3.00 a day for the more dangerous, below-surface work. And they wanted the company to recognize the union and the right of workers to organize and protect their economic interests through collective bargaining. Excitement rose among the miners, and the union went on strike ten days before the deadline for the company's response to the union proposal. The strike's jumpstart lost public sympathy for the miners and gave the advantage to U.S. Steel.

The company had other advantages as well. The WFM had few resources and was not prepared for a long strike. U.S. Steel, in contrast, did not need to mine immediately for ore. The ore boats that hauled iron ore to blast furnaces at Gary, Indiana, Youngstown, Ohio, and Pittsburgh, Pennsylvania, were not moving in midsummer 1907. Dockworkers in Duluth and Two Harbors were on strike, but the company was under no pressure; its stockpiles were adequate.

In addition, U.S. Steel could easily organize local business leaders, community officials, company management, maintenance workers, and other citizens against the outsiders (poorly paid and poorly educated miners). Local citizens and skilled trade workers were easily recruited as temporary sheriff's deputies, given arms to maintain order.

The conflict between U.S. Steel and the union quickly became a confrontation between the communities and the miners. Union activities heightened the tension. Strikers marched from town to town—from Eveleth to Hibbing to Chisholm, from mine to mine—calling meetings to protest conditions and urge other miners to join the strike. At the height of the conflict, some 45,000 men participated in or were idled by the strikes.

The strikes soon choked business activity on the range, further raising local ire. The anger of community leaders, striking miners, and armed citizens rose to a flashpoint. To avoid bloodshed, alarmed local authorities and mining companies asked Governor Johnson to send in the National Guard. Instead, Johnson took the train north to Duluth. He talked with the sheriff of St. Louis County, the mayor of Duluth, executives from U.S. Steel and Oliver Mining, and with delegations of striking dockworkers. The president of Oliver told the governor he would not negotiate with the striking miners. Neither would he concede on wages, hours, or other conditions.

Johnson then left Duluth to tour the Iron Range. He spoke with miners, local officials, and citizens. In Hibbing he went to the headquarters of the miners' union to speak with Teofilo Petriella, Italian immigrant-cum-head-of-the-Minnesota-WFM. The union wanted to avoid bloodshed, Petriella said.

In Eveleth, after visiting local union president John McNair and other miners, Johnson spoke at the town hall:

I do not see any occasion for the state to interfere at this time.
The men have a right to work. They have a right to organize

and to persuade others to quit work. But if a man wants to work and he and his employer agree that he shall work, he has a right to work, and no one has any right to stop him. If necessary, the state will protect men in their right to work.

The governor returned home satisfied there was no need for the National Guard.

In late July the dockworkers returned to their jobs, ending a two-and-a-half-week strike without gaining union recognition or increased pay. The iron miners continued their strike amid increased provocation by the mining companies. Petriella sent a telegram to Governor Johnson, asking him to prevent temporary deputies from disrupting meetings in union halls and to keep the mining companies from hiring armed guards to bring in replacement workers. The continued marches of striking miners brought community protests and renewed pleas for the National Guard.

Governor Johnson responded on August 2 with an official proclamation to citizens living on the Iron Range. "All persons, irrespective of their affiliation with labor unions or otherwise," he said, had a right to assemble peacefully in their own halls. Johnson directed public officials to prevent further upheaval. He said marching by miners constituted disturbance of the peace and forbade it. He warned the miners against trespassing on private mining property or attempting to keep anyone from working there. He prohibited union leaders' use of inflammatory language to incite violence and banned action by public officials that might excite the citizenry.

Upon violation of these conditions, Johnson warned (without saying how such violation might be determined), he would send in the National Guard. His proclamation deflated the tension, providing the WFM with reason to end the strike it already had lost. The industrial workers had only their physical labor to barter. Federal law would not require collective bargaining in good faith for another 30 years.

Nonetheless, labor achieved significant gains from its confrontation with U.S. Steel and the iron-mining companies. At the time, the governors of most of the states, especially in the middle and far west, routinely acceded to corporate appeals for National Guard troops and other police forces to break strikes as well as otherwise to control unions and organized labor. Johnson's refusal to use the National Guard was an early warning to U.S. Steel. He regarded both labor and management as respectable and responsible citizens.

Johnson's view that the law applied equally to the striking worker and to the owner of property was unique. Few leaders in the United States agreed with him, a condition setting the stage for the most violent confrontation between capital and labor in Minnesota's history and leading another of its governors to reconsider the role of the National Guard.

A quarter century after iron miners marched peacefully across the Iron Range, unemployment across the country and in Minnesota rose as the economy descended into the Great Depression. The conflict between American capital and labor reached its purest form in Minneapolis with the Teamsters' strike of 1934. The clash symbolized the romantic myth of rugged capitalism (almost leading to economic collapse) and demonstrated the value of pragmatic realism. Gov. Floyd B. Olson took steps beyond those of Governor Johnson to rebalance the system.[9]

The winter of 1933 was extraordinarily cold. November was ominous, and the Great Depression was settling in along with the cold weather. The business leaders of Minneapolis watched as President Franklin D. Roosevelt's New Deal took shape. Teamsters Local 547 began organizing Minneapolis coalyards that month under the procedures of the newly established National Labor Board (NLB), a federal agency authorized to negotiate voluntary agreements between companies and workers. The Teamsters sought recognition to represent drivers, helpers, and inside personnel working at 11 trucking firms delivering coal, the energy fuel of the time, to businesses and homes in Minneapolis. Rather than agree to collective bargaining, the trucking companies formed the Citizens Alliance. The Alliance represented the coalyards in discussions with the NLB, but it would not recognize the Teamsters' Union.

Through the winter the Alliance sought to widen the conflict. It enlisted Minneapolis and St. Paul companies to join in demonstrating opposition to the Teamsters' campaign to organize firms in the Twin Cities. In March the Alliance warned Minneapolis employers of a possible strike. By the end of April the Alliance had grown to include 166 firms.

The battle lines were set. Instead of dealing with 11 trucking firms, the Teamsters found themselves pitted against the Minneapolis and St. Paul business establishment, a situation with potential for engulfing the community in a class war. Buoyed by the larger business community, the Alliance rejected the Teamsters' request for recognition to represent workers at the 11 trucking firms. Members of Local 574 voted on May 16 to strike.

Three days later, on May 19, the strikers formed picket lines in the Minneapolis market district, around the loading docks of the trucking firms. When the pickets ignored their orders to disperse, city police, aided by special deputies armed with clubs, drove them away. The Alliance had recruited the deputies from families in the business community, and the police had sworn them in.

The strikers returned May 21 and fought a pitched battle resulting in injuries to 37 of their membership. The next day, May 22, the battle resumed. Strikers, armed with clubs and iron pipes, drove the police and special deputies from the market district in the "Battle of Deputies Run." Two special deputies died in the fight.

Gov. Floyd B. Olson, watching the conflict from the Minnesota State Capitol in St. Paul, stepped in on May 23 to propose a truce and offer mediation. Two days of tense discussion ensued, and on May 25,

Olson finally brokered an agreement between the Teamsters and the Alliance. The Teamsters believed they had reached an agreement on wages and working conditions with the 11 trucking companies but that the Alliance had not recognized them as the representative of the workers. The Alliance contended it had agreed to mediate with the National Labor Board through Governor Olson and that it had not recognized the Teamsters at all.

During June, the Teamsters found ample reason to believe the trucking companies were not living up to their agreement. In some instances, wages paid were under the stated amount. In others, non-union members received higher wages than did Teamsters. As July began, Local 547 charged that the employers had failed to honor the agreement mediated by Governor Olson.

The Teamsters' strike started anew on Wednesday, July 18, blocking trucking. City officials warned that the strike would strangle deliveries to neighborhood grocery stores. A single truck, said by police to carry food and medical supplies, drove through the picket lines July 18 and 19 to test the Teamsters' resolve. Police and special deputies watched nervously as the strikers allowed the truck to pass. Again on Friday, July 20, the truck, armed with a sign announcing it carried food and medical supplies, proceeded. But *Minneapolis Star* photographs showed that the first truck was empty. Now a Teamsters' truck carrying union members raced into the street, cutting off the "bait" truck. Police waiting on the sidewalks with pistols and rifles opened fire on the Teamster truck. Two strikers died in the hail of bullets, and more than 30 others were wounded that "Bloody Friday." Subsequent investigation showed police had staged the incident to incite the strikers to violence.

The conflict shocked Olson and left the community shaken. The governor's appeal to the Minneapolis police chief to stop incurring violence met with rejection; the chief said the Alliance wanted police escorts for more trucks. Tension mounted as the city waited for the next police move. Governor Olson declared martial law on July 26, and the Minnesota National Guard took control of Minneapolis. A system of permits allowed limited deliveries of food and fuel. Strikers could no longer interfere with the shipments.

Martial law could not continue indefinitely, especially as the National Guard soon increased the number of permits. Olson was stymied. The Alliance refused to recognize the Teamsters' Union, and the Teamster leadership could not back down. Now the Alliance challenged the governor's edict with a lawsuit asking the federal court to revoke martial law.

While preparing for the court hearing on the Alliance petition, Olson also was working behind the scenes. The banking system had collapsed as the Great Depression deepened. Credit, the lifeblood of commerce and business, was tight. President Roosevelt had declared a banking moratorium, and Congress authorized the Reconstruction Finance Corporation (RFC) to supply credit to shuttered banks. The Teamsters charged the RFC with bankrolling the Alliance. Since key members of the Alliance were Minneapolis bankers, Olson sought to enjoin the Minneapolis RFC office in pressuring the business community to end the strike.

A special three-judge panel heard the petition to end martial law on August 6. Governor Olson, representing himself, told the panel that martial law is not subject to judicial review. "The responsibility of government is . . . to protect the lives of all people. To rule otherwise, the court has to find that the martial law order did not contribute to that end," he said. If the court revoked martial law, he would withdraw the National Guard, and he would not accept responsibility for the consequences.[10]

Governor Olson left the hearing to go to Rochester, Minnesota, to meet with President Roosevelt, scheduled to speak on August 8 at the Mayo Clinic. While Olson met with Roosevelt, Teamsters representatives also met with Louis Howe, the president's top political advisor.

The Teamsters asked Howe to bring Jesse Jones, the RFC director, to the rescue. They wanted Jones to contact the Minneapolis bankers who were running the regional RFC office. They said the issue in the strike was collective bargaining, emphasizing that one word from Jones could settle the strike. A day later Jones called the Minneapolis RFC office, setting in motion events that would do so.

Civil strife still threatened the Twin Cities on August 11, when the federal judges agreed unanimously that "we do not believe we would be justified in invalidating the governor's proclamation of martial law." The judges said, "If the courts assume to interfere, [Olson] will consider himself relieved of any further responsibility." The jurists prudently surmised that while the "federal government could intervene, violence and bloodshed could reoccur before an order could be obtained. Issuance of a preliminary injunction might result in a more serious breakdown than had yet occurred."

The three-judge panel condemned Olson, imputing the governor's motives were suspect. "We believe Olson is coercing the companies to accept a [negotiated] settlement," the judges said. "But we do not feel justified in intervening when there is no clear and convincing proof the governor is violating his oath of office. The governor must bear responsibility for his actions."[11]

Business, government, and labor learned important lessons from the Teamsters' strike. The business community, in making the strike a battleground for class conflict, caused wiser heads nationally to recognize that organized labor must be brought within the social consensus. Collective bargaining thus became a legal instrument to preserve comity. Minneapolis government never again became a pawn in an ideological conflict, and the community looked beyond the business sector for political leadership. The electorate has not since the Teamsters' strike chosen someone from the business community as mayor. Labor henceforth was active in local politics so as to deter law enforcement from acting as a weapon of the business sector.

American government discovered the will to discipline the business community in recognizing that the right of workers to bargain collectively for wages and working conditions must be guaranteed by law. In 1935 Congress codified the rights of organized labor by adopting the Wagner Act, as much a testament to Governor Olson as to President Roosevelt. The Wagner Act recognized collective bargaining as a peaceful process bringing labor and its goals of economic justice within the rule of law of democratic governance, thus replacing a militant labor force's radical behavior with a conservative tradition (legal action).

In 1959 the final chapter on industrial conflict in Minnesota arose over the same collective bargaining issues in the strike at the Wilson plant in Albert Lea. Governor Freeman acted in that situation upon the community's request to restore local order before the loss of lives. On December 12, Wilson and Company challenged his December 9 martial-law decree in the same federal court in which the three-judge panel had deferred to Governor Olson's martial-law edict. Two of the three federal district court judges who ruled in the Teamsters' strike were on the December 16 panel hearing arguments about Freeman's similar action. Even greater irony prevailed: The attorneys representing Wilson also were among those who had represented the Citizens Alliance in seeking to overturn Olson's martial-law decision. Now they sought for Wilson what they had not been able to get 25 years earlier for the 116 companies of the Alliance.

Wilson's record of hostile labor relations also stemmed from the 1930s. In 1937 the company rejected collective bargaining. In 1938, it was cited for violating the Wagner Act by establishing a company union in the Albert Lea plant. In 1942 Wilson refused to sign a labor-contract agreement until President Roosevelt threatened to halt the federal government's purchase of meat supplies from the firm.

After World War II, the UPWA emerged through aggressive organizing as the dominant union representing packinghouse workers. In

1947 UPWA proposed its first master (industrywide) contract for negotiations on wages and working conditions. Meat companies joined in a united front to avoid negotiating separately, rejected the master contract, setting up a test of wills with the union. A bitter strike involving four Minnesota meat plants, including Wilson's in Albert Lea, ensued. Gov. Luther Youngdahl used National Guard troops to keep the Swift and Cudahy plants open in St. Paul and Newport, another instance of a Minnesota governor directing the National Guard to defuse a labor-management conflict. The strike ended after five months, with the UPWA gaining its master contract. In Albert Lea the strike was especially bitter because Wilson actively recruited strikebreakers. The company was the last to sign the master contract.

Twelve years later, all the meat companies but Wilson signed the renegotiated master contract. Contract negotiations with Wilson stretched through the summer of 1959 without resolution, setting the stage for Governor Freeman's decision to call out the National Guard. In late August, union members in five Wilson plants across the United States voted to strike. Freeman and Iowa's Gov. Herschel Loveless offered state conciliation services. Wilson rejected the offers.

The company fought not only the Albert Lea union but also the city's government. The Wilson plant, which had remained in a township that refused annexation as Albert Lea grew around the plant, was dumping plant effluence into Lake Albert Lea. The polluted lake was off-limits to swimmers for reasons of health. The city was suing the company, which paid no local taxes, to cease dumping and for cleanup costs. The township, its residents mostly Wilson employees, had no police force of its own and had to pay the city for protection.

As the strike continued through September and October, the city suffered economically. Union members earned an average $90 per week from Wilson, while the UPWA paid strike benefits of only ten dollars. With more than 1,100 workers on strike, the losses to local business reached more than $100,000 weekly.

As the strike entered its eighth week in early November, the weight of history brought unavoidable pressure to bear. The memory of earlier violence, the mutual distrust of company and workers, the frustration of local businesses, the company's environmental behavior, and Wilson's efforts to evade support of Albert Lea contributed to a rising level of tension. Into this atmosphere Wilson introduced an explosive element—a campaign of psychological terror aimed at workers and families. The company obtained a temporary injunction on November 19 from Minnesota District Judge John Cahill to prevent mass picketing at the plant gates. Six days later, on November 25, Wilson sent letters to the strikers, threatening to fire those who did not return to work and replace them with nonunion workers.

At Wilson's request, Judge Cahill delayed a November 26 hearing on the temporary injunction until November 30. After hearing the arguments, Cahill said he would rule December 21 on Wilson's motion for a permanent injunction. Wilson began recruiting strikebreakers the next day, December 1, and sent union members another letter on December 5, repeating its threats. The workers, with reason, believed the company intended to break the union. By December 6 several hundred strikebreakers worked at the plant.

Union members watched as Wilson maneuvered Judge Cahill into delaying his ruling on the injunction for almost a month. The delay gave Wilson more time to break the strike. To union members, the delay in justice was justice denied. The court appeared to be in the company's pocket. In the face of sporadic violence on December 6, Judge Cahill called Governor Freeman to warn him that the conflict in Albert Lea was spinning out of control.

A day later Freeman sent State Labor Conciliator Johnson and State Highway Safety Director Sieben to monitor the situation at the Wilson plant. On December 8 Freeman urged both management and the union to meet with Johnson. The union accepted the plea, but Wilson and Company rejected it.[12]

James Cooney, president of Wilson, took the train north from Chicago on December 12 to meet with Governor Freeman. An imperious figure, described by reporters as "genial but uncommunicative," Cooney strode into the room serving as an antechamber for the governor's office.[13] Amid the flash of cameras, he entered Freeman's office, emerging only ten minutes later to express his disappointment at the governor's refusal to withdraw his order for martial law.

Federal mediator Charles Olson in Chicago announced on December 15, 1959, that Wilson had agreed to resume its collective bargaining with the union, broken off by the company on October 29 of that year. Talks would take place in January in Chicago, with a possible first meeting on December 28, 1959. The announcement let everybody know that Wilson had abandoned its strategy of breaking the union.[14]

The hearing on Wilson's petition for the return of its plant took place in federal court December 16. Wilson's attorneys denied any need to close the plant and argued the National Guard could have maintained law and order. Governor Freeman told the judges that "men who had worked in the plant for years, who had their homes, their families, and all of their relatives there, were suddenly told to come back to work or there will be no work for you." He dismissed Wilson's arguments, pointing out that the company's attorneys were not in Albert Lea and could not know the situation. Freeman said city and county officials held a different view and emphasized that he had acted prudently in sending representatives to monitor the scene. "My decision," Freeman said, "was to see that whatever lawlessness there [was] on both sides be stopped."

The court said it would rule shortly but set no date. Three days later, on December 19, Wilson resumed collective bargaining with the UPWA. The decision to resume pulled the thorn from the conflict and served both the economic and judicial interests of the company. If Wilson delayed its return to the bargaining table, the federal court would confront the same condition it had faced in the Teamsters' strike—whether a decision for the company would be perceived as supporting the refusal of owners to bargain collectively. Freeman had said he acted to prevent lawlessness on both sides. If people died upon the withdrawal of troops, would others blame the court?

Further, Wilson was losing an estimated $250,000 for each week the plant was closed. Stockholders would ask about what management could gain by fighting the UPWA over a contract that Wilson's competitors, including its larger rivals Swift and Cudahy, had signed months earlier.

Since martial law extended only to the township and not to Albert Lea, the city returned to relative quiet as it awaited the federal court ruling. In the immediate sway of martial law plus the resumption of bargaining, vandalism in the city and county ceased. Tension among union members eased as the martial-law decree appeared to balance a perceived court bias for the company. Further, the closing of the plant had thrust Wilson into national headlines; the company could no longer maintain hostile relations with workers without running the risk of a national boycott of Wilson products. The corollary was that Freeman also appeared in headlines nationally, and editorial writers in every major newspaper battered him mercilessly for closing the plant.

The federal court handed down its ruling on December 24, ordering Freeman to end martial law and return the plant to Wilson. "The governor possesses no absolute authority to declare martial law," the three-judge panel concluded. "The authority can be sustained only in situations of dire necessity, and we are convinced that situation had not yet arisen in Freeborn County."

The court, as in its judgment of Governor Olson's actions in the Teamsters' strike, agreed that martial law was an executive power not to be extinguished by judicial decree. Neither did the court limit martial law by requiring prior judicial consent for its use. Looking at conditions after the fact, the court said it was not convinced of the existence of "dire necessity" in this case—that is, if the court had been governor it might have acted differently.

The court examined only two situations in which a governor in Minnesota had declared martial law in a violent class conflict. In Minneapolis, martial law had been declared after citizens were killed; no deaths had occurred in Albert Lea. The court did not explain the conditions constituting "dire necessity," a slender thread on which to distinguish its reluctance to intervene in the Teamsters' strike. A more robust explanation would be that Governor Olson had been involved in civil strife that remained unresolved when the three-judge panel ruled on martial law, while Wilson's attorneys, having gone to school on the Teamsters' strike, suggested the company would lose its case unless it returned to collective bargaining. The definition of "dire necessity" escaped public attention, however. In both the Teamsters' strike in Minneapolis and the Wilson strike in Albert Lea, collective bargaining as a peaceful process depended on the good faith of both parties. In the Teamsters' strike the Alliance relied on the court to allow it to break the strike and the union. In the Wilson strike the company quickly resumed collective bargaining, thus relieving the court of taking sides in the bargaining process.

The arguments of the three-judge panel in the December 24, 1959, decision differed from those presented in the August 11, 1934, decision only in tone and in the introduction of the concept of "dire necessity." The 1934 ruling betrayed the jurists' discomfort with community violence still seething, while the 1959 ruling exuded a calm reflection that Freeman had restored community order so as to pull the thorn (the company's refusal to bargain with the union) from the conflict. "Dire necessity" was not so much a legal concept as a phrase completing the court's unfinished denunciation of Governor Olson. In 1934 the jurists said, "We do not believe we would be justified in invalidating the governor's proclamation [without] clear and convincing proof the governor is violating his oath of office." In 1959 the jurists added the phrase "dire necessity" as the judicial test of "convincing proof" when an oath of office is violated.

"Dire necessity" is not judicial guidance but rather a judicial warrant for the court to intervene in displeasing executive actions. Had violence followed the withdrawal of the National Guard in Albert Lea around the Wilson plant, Governor Freeman again would have proclaimed martial law to restore order. The Minnesota Constitution nowhere specifies the proclamation of martial law "only under circumstances of dire necessity."[15]

The court acknowledged "dire necessity" as a warrant for intervention when the jurists were unable to provide specific criteria to company management or future governors for applying the use of martial law. For example, in examining Governor Johnson's approach to the request of mining companies for use of the National Guard to suppress striking miners, the court would have determined that Johnson not only sent observers but also visited the scene himself, talking with miners and mine owners. Johnson decided not to intervene. The court also would have known from its exposure to the Teamsters' strike in Minneapolis that Governor Olson had observers on the scene and was himself in regular communication with city officials. In considering the use of martial law, both governors had sought to act only after seeking sufficient information.

Another criteria with which to judge appropriate use of martial law is the perception of local officials, in their assessment of or control of conditions, of the need for martial law. Local officials urged Governor Johnson to use martial law to control striking miners, but he decided National Guard troops were not necessary. Governor Olson acted when local officials clearly had lost control of the city and, further, endangered the community by inciting violence. Governor Freeman acted on the advice and counsel of local officials to stabilize a situation they perceived was beyond their control. Gathering information is a prudent action prior to making decisions.

Another criteria for "dire necessity" is whether a governor has demonstrated prudence in approaching a situation that might benefit from martial law. For example, Freeman took an evenhanded approach to the dispute between the company and the union. When negotiations first broke off, he proposed that both parties use the services of the state labor conciliator. Rejection by the company of a reasonable and prudent offer to resolve the dispute peacefully limited the options available to Freeman when the dispute spiraled out of control.

"Dire necessity," however, is a moot concept, forever consigned to a hypothetical world. The court chose not to define the term since, as with pornography, there is no legal definition. A governor will always ignore it. The state constitution defines the authority for declaring martial law as an instrument of police powers for emergency use by the chief executive acting as civil commander of military forces.

In failing to offer guidelines for evaluating "dire necessity," the court conceded it could not interfere with the use of martial law. Instead it was pleading with Governor Freeman not to embarrass the court by raising the constitutional question of the separation of powers. On its face, the decision appears to advise that only upon loss of life should a governor take the action that would have saved those lives. Since no governor or court would consciously endorse an immoral act—accepting the loss of life when other, less horrific options are available—the decision recognizes that the use of martial law is a political decision. Minnesota's constitution authorizes only the executive to make this kind of political decision. In doing so, the constitution recognizes the need for authority to act promptly in the public interest.

The rule of law relating to the effect of industrialization on social and economic policy could change only as quickly as statutory provisions or judicial attitudes could accommodate the conflicting demands of civil society. In Minnesota the changes came rapidly and with dislocation. In the Teamsters' strike, the role of law-enforcement agencies in inciting violence did not become general knowledge (that might provide guidance in sifting out judicial or statutory policies) until long after the restoration of order. In that instance, the imposition of martial law was a prudent use of constitutional authority by executive power, however sourly the court may have viewed Olson as a politician sensitive to the thrust of social change. The decision in Albert Lea reflects the inertia of the judicial system, which also protects social stability, and can lead judges to ignore the social contexts in which the two events occurred.

Freeman at Albert Lea represents the use of executive authority by a governor enmeshed in the political changes of Minnesota at the beginning of a new social and economic era, the period following World War II. Two new political forces, neither based on the purely economic conflicts generated by industrialization, dominated Minnesota politics then. One was returning war veterans (like Freeman) unlikely to view their sacrifices as justifying the abusive corporate behavior toward workers that Wilson personified. Collective bargaining was the peaceful option to corporate warfare in the workplace.

Equally as powerful were women, the benefits of their long struggle for suffrage delayed first by the Great Depression and then by World War II. Wives joined husbands on the picket line because the company's behavior threatened family, children, home, and place in the community. All were at stake. Gaining the right to vote promised women economic security and community stability for which they would no longer have to rely on picket line alone. For women, collective bargaining also was the peaceful option to workplace conflict.

Veterans and women led the shift of the Minnesota electorate in postwar perspective of the role of government. Freeman, as governor and leader of the DFL, gave shape and identity to the shift in defining the context of Albert Lea. He noted:

The vast majority of the American people have only the fruits of their labor to consider as property. And as the industrial worker establishes a record of years of service, he has established a recognizable claim to his job. If we are to maintain individual rights and freedoms in our mass culture, should legal protection also be extended to individual rights?

The answer, of course, is a political judgment that citizens as voters must make as the economy grows, the workplace changes, and the definition of labor adjusts with the economic system. Freeman's action in Albert Lea clearly defined the DFL in the 1950s. This was a promise that in future economic conflicts between workers and corporate owners the DFL would support worker rights, individual freedoms, and democratic governance.

The events involving Albert Lea, Wilson, and the United Packinghouse Workers Union seemingly do not have the passion and sweep of the Iron Range conflict or the bloody drama of the confrontation between organized labor and the Minneapolis establishment. But to say that alone is to misread the events in Albert Lea. The pain and agony of families were no less real or less moving on a smaller stage. While events on the Iron Range and in Minneapolis may have anticipated a better future through social change, Albert Lea symbolized the tragedy of craftsmen unable to achieve the promise of the American dream.

The strike ended with the resumption of collective bargaining in January 1960. Management and unions could not agree on the issue of jobs. Wilson had promised permanent employment to strikebreakers, and the union insisted on the return of union members to their jobs. The company and the union agreed to binding arbitration in April 1960. The arbitration panel reached the Solomonic decision for awarding jobs in the Albert Lea plant by seniority. As all union members had more seniority, the settlement rejected the long-term goal of the Wilson Company to break the union. Shortly thereafter, the Wilson board "promoted" James Cooney to chairmanship of a board committee on long-term planning, removing him as chief executive officer. Twenty-three years after the Albert Lea strike, in 1983, Wilson and Company declared bankruptcy. UPWA merged with the Amalgamated Meat Cutters and Butcher Workmen in 1968.

The events in Albert Lea marked the start of meat-industry changes to which American society continues to adjust. Packing plants introduced automation and other technological processing measures and replaced industrial craftsworkers with low-wage, unskilled workers. Packinghouses closed in Chicago, St. Paul, Omaha, and Kansas City as packers moved to new, bigger plants built close to feedlots raising tens of thousands of cattle and hogs to slaughter weight. The shift immediately left thousands of skilled workers unemployed. And individual farmers and growers increasingly must choose between going out of business and becoming contract growers who invest in growout facilities for piecemeal payment.

These changes also affect the health of the American citizen, rendered in health-care costs never present in the calculations of food-processor profit-and-loss statements. The upward trend of food-borne illnesses in the United States has gone uninterrupted in the past half-century. Meat and poultry, and food products containing meat and poultry, are the principal source of food-poisoning bacteria. The loss of packinghouse workers with the training, experience, and professionalism to care about the quality and safety of their products is a factor in that trend.

*Gov. Orville L. Freeman delivered his third inaugural address on January 7,
1959, following his campaign during the Minnesota Centennial. He needed
the leadership and votes of both houses to finance his hopes for the state.*

—6—

The Battle over Withholding

Some 20 men gathered to discuss taxes with Governor-elect Freeman on the evening of December 9, 1954. The topic had been noticeably absent as an issue during the 1954 campaign that brought Freeman and the DFL to power on November 5. Now the party controlled the House of Representatives by a majority of one. Freeman and many of those in the room, half of them legislators, had been elected to answer the question he now asked. "How should I propose to close a budget deficit estimated to be $40 million for the 1956–57 biennium?"

"Start slashing," Sen. Harold Schultz, a Liberal from a St. Paul labor district, proposed immediately. His constituents were worried more about taxes than about services. "They just don't want any more taxes," he said.

"People are tax-conscious," Freeman agreed. "But organized groups are program-conscious." The exchange embodied political leaders' eternal tax dilemma. Elections occur on a shorter timetable than do social change and program growth. People vote against taxes, and when services require more funding than is available, politicians usually equivocate. As a result, public services suffer, organized groups protest, and voters turn out the politicians who allowed the crisis.

A significant number of Freeman voters said they voted against the Republican incumbent, C. Elmer Anderson. They told pollsters after the election that the Republicans were not doing the job they expected. It was time for a change. That belief had been the theme of Freeman's campaign, and the voters expected answers from the victor. Participants in the December 9 meeting would have been upset had Freeman not consulted them. But they shuffled uneasily, not unlike children who would rather be anywhere but a family prayer meeting.

The easy answers came first. Someone proposed shifting programs from funding streams, where revenues were short, to other, more plentiful streams. The Minnesota Legislature over the years had compartmentalized tax revenues so as to direct funding to specific program areas. For instance, income-tax receipts went to public schools, iron-ore taxes to education and the University of Minnesota (U of M), gasoline taxes to highways, and general revenues to state government programs and services. But as another observed, the DFL had opposed earlier attempts to raid those revenue preserves, even building a constituency around that position. With the DFL in the governor's office and the House of Representatives, the shoe was on the other foot.

"We must assume present taxes are equitable," another legislator said unconvincingly, "and increase them all a little."

Others proposed passing the buck. "Orv should submit a budget balanced by putting new taxes on only several sources," one said, describing an earlier Anderson proposal.

"That was dead the day it was introduced," came the reply. "Orv should propose a spending program and ask the legislature to provide the funds."

Freeman dismissed the suggestion. "I was elected to lead," he said.

In the midst of the discussion of new taxes versus cuts in programs, one top DFL official felt more comfortable proposing new spending. "What we have to do is consolidate labor support by improving unemployment and workmen's compensation. The AFL and CIO are already with us. But we need some middle groups. We should do something about old-age assistance."

A legislator recalled that a bill introduced by Liberals in 1953 had called for a pay-as-you-go system to collect income taxes on payroll earnings—a system of withholding. Freeman said he knew of the system, that it would temporarily increase collections through a "windfall" effect. The federal government had adopted withholding during World War II to more efficiently collect revenues for waging the war.

Freeman thanked the participants for coming together. In the days following, he met with business leaders, who advised him to call for reduced taxes to improve the business climate in Minnesota. They offered no suggestions on program cuts. Advocacy groups also met with the governor-elect. The state mental-health advisory committee extracted a commitment for a psychiatrists' training program. Freeman reassured several education groups and organizations that he would fulfill his pledge to raise state per-pupil school aid to $92.

Freeman met December 18 and 19 with his key budget advisors, Arthur Naftalin, commissioner of administration, and Walter Heller, U of M professor of economics.[1] Freeman asked for a budget calling for new taxes in certain areas, increased iron-ore and some excise taxes, and payroll withholding. He made his final decision on January 2, 1954, just two days before delivery of his inaugural message.

As the December 18 meeting ended, Freeman asked Naftalin and Heller to think about how to address revenue needs two years hence. Revenue surpluses had delayed the day of reckoning since the end of World War II. Now they were gone. Program spending was increasing faster than revenue, and the future was clear. Simply maintaining services would create an even larger deficit for the 1957 biennium.

The problem was not complicated, but it was unavoidable. The baby boom strained school facilities inadequately maintained during and after the war. New schools were necessary. Higher education could not keep up with enrollment. And with half its citizens living in urban areas, Minnesota was no longer a rural state. The suburbs were growing, and people expected state government to do more. They expected it to build more roads, repair deteriorating buildings and construct new facilities, improve conservation, adopt mental-health reforms, do more to help the elderly, and ensure the best possible education for its youth.

During the previous decade, state expenditures had more than doubled. In the 1943–45 biennium, the legislature appropriated $385 million. Ten years later, state spending reached $800 million. Tax revenues initially had kept pace with the cost of government, but the tax structure could not produce the revenue for postwar needs. Revenue surpluses were gone by 1955. A crisis was at hand.

Freeman believed he had been elected to lead. Leadership, he saw now, involved not only the task of convincing Minnesota voters that services could be provided for an urban society but also that of reforming the tax structure. It had to be one that voters would support. It had to uphold the dreams and ambitions of an urban citizenry.

Minnesota in 1955 already had one of the most progressive tax systems in the nation. Adopted in the 1930s, it rested on the policy that taxes must be paid by those most able to do so. Putting income-tax revenues into education, for example, recognized that those who benefit from education can afford to pay the cost of educating those who follow. One of just 16 states without a general sales tax, Minnesota relied instead on income and severance taxes. One of every four dollars of state tax revenues came from excise and consumer taxes. Only four other states took less than Minnesota from this source.

The challenge for Freeman and the DFL was to strengthen and make this progressive system more flexible. Freeman and the DFL opposed a general sales tax, arguing that a regressive tax system would fall more heavily on moderate- and lower-income individuals and families. As Freeman and his advisors analyzed state finances, they realized that the tax system necessary to fund state-government programs would be the central political issue of the years ahead.

Leaders of industry and business, other interest groups, and the press were no less aware of the looming struggle. Newspapers throughout the state called for a sales tax, as did trade and industry groups and associations. No Republican called openly for a sales tax. But the GOP and the DFL both understood that the funding crisis was an open invitation to initiating one. Some newspaper editors believed and wrote, "A sales tax is inevitable."

Quickly grasping that the Republicans and Conservatives would impose a regressive tax system as the price of progress, Freeman rejected that argument. His comments to Naftalin and Heller at the end of the December 18 meeting demonstrate that he had begun to chew on a political strategy for tax policy. It might be advisable, he said, to divert future iron-ore taxes to immediate education needs. Revenues from iron-ore taxes were dedicated to two trust funds—a permanent school fund and a permanent university fund. Earnings from the first went to primary and secondary schools, while earnings from the latter were available only to the U of M. Both funds bulged, but even modest inflation would depreciate their value substantially within ten or 20 years. Using current revenues destined for those funds would ensure access to their full value before inflation.

Capping the dedicated funds at current levels would allow use of future income for current expenditures. But voters in the 1956 election first must approve a constitutional amendment authorizing such a change in policy. Freeman asked for estimates of potential revenues from the change. Within days, he learned that at least $20 million would be available for the 1957–59 biennium. Raising the iron-ore tax rate from 11 to 15 percent would provide even more. Capping the trust funds would ease pressure on the legislature to raise taxes in 1957, a scenario tax experts now said was unavoidable.

Freeman also told Naftalin and Heller that he hoped to use a portion of the withholding windfall to increase by five dollars the ten-dollar tax credit allowed taxpayers for each dependent.[2] The low- and moderate-income families constituting the greatest proportion of the tax base would receive most of the windfall. This further strengthened the progressive aspect of the tax system.

Freeman recognized that withholding would become a symbol for the income tax in the political debate over tax policy. Withholding simplifies payment as well as collection of taxes, easing the burden of an annual lump-sum payment into more frequent but smaller installments. Payroll deductions also ensure the fair treatment of every wage earner, as well decrease tax cheating, increase revenue without raising rates, and provide fairer taxpayer-sharing of responsibility for services.

The debate over tax policy contrasted withholding with the imposition of a new (sales) tax. Freeman laid bare the negative features of the sales tax, creating an insurmountable obstacle for its advocates. His best arguments posited that a consumption tax shifts the tax burden to families and individuals, taking a larger proportion of their income, particularly for low- and moderate-income groups. In 1950, the U.S. Census Bureau found median income in Minnesota was $3,163, or about $60 a week, slightly below the national average.

Introducing withholding as a proxy for the income tax put tax policy at the center of political debate. Advocates of the sales tax could succeed in imposing a regressive tax system only if there were a funding crisis—that is, only if the Conservatives could foment an impasse solvable only through a sales tax. Freeman could not prevent an immediate crisis, but his suggestion for a progressive income tax collected in small amounts through withholding made the sales tax the least-attractive political alternative. The way to avoid a future crisis was through a long-term income-tax policy addressing future social and economic needs in Minnesota.

This strategy guided the governor-elect even before his inauguration. As 1954 wound down, Freeman met at the Minnesota State Capitol with the preeminent education lobby, the Education Coordinating Committee. He said he would honor his campaign pledge by proposing to raise per-pupil aid to $92. The increase would cost about $15 million for the 1956–57 biennium, he explained, to be paid with half of the withholding windfall.

Freeman recalled that education groups traditionally had avoided recommending tax sources to the legislature. He described as irresponsible the practice of supporting increased spending without willingness to support greater taxes. His words hit home. The chair of the coalition said the group had never before supported a tax plan. But he promised Freeman that education groups would support withholding.

Freeman then revealed he was considering a proposal to amend the state constitution so as to cap the permanent school trust fund and use future iron-ore tax revenues for current education programs. Though the lobby had always supported continuation of the current trust-fund policy, none of the education advocates raised an objection.

Tax-policy-decision day—January 2—was anticlimactic. Freeman already had decided to propose withholding, a measure that would provide the funds to raise per-pupil aid to $92 dollars a year. Enough revenue would remain to increase income-tax credits for dependents. Freeman told Naftalin and Heller he would also propose capping the school trust funds, which they said would allow the state easily to meet the $92-per-pupil aid in the 1957–59 biennium. And it could put off future education-cost issues for at least four years. The governor could use that time to develop a long-range tax program for Minnesota. Raising iron-ore tax rates, and to a lesser degree those on wine and beer, cigarettes, and other consumption items, would close an estimated $50-million revenue gap for the biennium.[3]

Freeman invited the Liberal legislative leadership to preview his budget proposals and make last-minute recommendations. Apprehension evident at the December 18 meeting apparently had faded. The House leaders sent word back to Tom Hughes, Freeman's executive secretary, that they would be better able to get the governor's program through without too much participation in its formation.

Freeman took office on January 5, 1955. He was 36 years old. At the inaugural ceremony, his wife, Jane, and their two young children, Constance and Michael, sat proudly in the seats of honor in the balcony opposite the speaker's dais. With the press looking on, Mike whispered, "Remember, mother, don't yawn."

Five days later, on the eve of his first budget message, Governor Freeman met with department heads, most of them holdovers from the Anderson administration. Facing almost certain replacement in the coming months, they nevertheless would testify before the legislative appropriation committees in support of budget proposals for their programs.

"Our decisions on the budget have been difficult," Freeman said. "Tax dollars are short. The public is for lower taxes, but I don't think that is right. We will not knuckle under, but we must all educate the public in regard to needs and to the value of state programs. We must give efficient and honest administration.

"You may have your disappointments," he told the department heads. None had seen the budget, but all had a general sense of what was coming:

> I hope you will make allowances. You will have to justify your requests before the legislature. If you come out a little better, all right. But use tact and understanding, so that it does not appear we are fighting each other, with the commissioner of administration somewhere in between.

Governor Freeman proposed a biennial budget of $335 million, including a $50-million increase in new taxes for the 1955–57 biennium. Education costs accounted for $31 million of the increase in taxes, half to meet a deficit in the income-tax school fund and half to raise per-pupil assistance from $80 to $92 dollars a year. The general revenue fund, supporting all other state programs and services, would require an additional $19 million in revenues. Withholding was to provide additional revenues for much of the increase in educational spending, while increases in excise taxes and iron-ore taxes took care of other educational needs, including the University of Minnesota. It would provide as well for state services and programs.

Senate Conservatives, led by Donald O. Wright and Gordon Rosenmeier, rejected withholding and sought to lure Freeman and the DFL into a special session over taxes. They hoped to depict the new governor as continuing the behavior of the Farmer-Labor Party, discredited a generation earlier. Still, the two camps reached a compromise, increasing revenues by $24 million in new revenues but without raising income-tax rates.[4] The agreement, reached at the last minute, provided an $82-per-pupil aid payment, an increase of two dollars. The 1955 session dodged an extended conflict over tax policy. Freeman quietly buried Republican hopes for a replay of the 1937 Farmer-Labor disaster.

Even before the 1955 session, Freeman had started building bridges to the business community. As governor-elect he went on a speaking trip to Wall Street to extol the virtues of Minnesota. The legislative session reinforced his sense of urgency for tax reform, and a meeting with J. Cameron Thomson, chair of the board of Northwest Bancorporation, led to discussions of the impact of taxes in Minnesota on industry, business development, and job creation. After the 1955 legislature adjourned sine die, the two agreed on July 15 "to conduct a thorough and impartial study of the Minnesota tax structure."[5] And Governor Freeman established the Governor's Minnesota Tax Study Committee. Thomson agreed to serve as its chair.

A blue-ribbon panel of 20 citizens with official alternates representing business (seven members), labor (seven members), and agriculture (four members) emerged after consultation with groups in those sectors. Two members from academia—Walter Heller, regarded a top U.S. tax expert, and Francis M. Boddy of the U of M department of business development—also served. None was a member of the legislature. Each sector, other than the university, nominated its own representatives. Seven economists and tax experts, all but two from outside Minnesota, provided research, and there was staff support as well. The cost of the study eventually reached $70,000, with business and industry contributing $60,000, labor and agriculture the rest. Francis Boddy, U of M professor of economics, described the committee as making "the first large-scale basic study . . . by a group that didn't have the answers in advance, really independent study."[6]

Freeman had no involvement once the committee began its work on November 5, 1955. He had named as its executive director Kenneth M. Anderson, a professor of taxation at the university law school and a GOP precinct worker. Anderson served until June 1956; Stanley Kinyon, also of the law-school faculty, replaced him.

Heller said, "What was really remarkable was that the findings were adopted unanimously after some indications the committee might fall apart on the issue of the sales tax." He told Thomson that the sales-tax discussion had to wait as the committee

> peeled off one issue after another that wasn't controversial, and then we got into the quasi-controversial ones and we got unanimous agreement. Everybody had such a stake in making the thing go . . . It was possible to achieve agreement on the sales tax.[7]

The committee neither supported nor opposed a sales tax. In a delicately fashioned compromise, it said,

The time is near at hand in this state when the legislature must grant local communities authority to levy new non-property taxes of substantial revenue potential. [If not,] local government will have to appeal to the legislature for further and substantial grants-in-aid, or for further sharing of state-collected taxes, or both.

The committee decided not to propose new revenue sources to provide for those needs, opting instead to treat the question of a tax instrument as a technical issue. Staff recommended that policymakers consider a sales tax, a value-added tax, or increases in the personal income tax. The committee staff made a dispassionate case for a system of credits structured so that the sales tax would be progressive at low and middle incomes and proportionate in those higher.[8]

Following his reelection in 1956, Freeman used the momentum from the accolades given the Governor's Tax Study Committee to make withholding the centerpiece of his legislative proposals to the 1957 legislature. House Liberals, now with a seven-vote margin, moved quickly to adopt the DFL programs, sending a tax proposal to the Senate early in the three-month session. As in 1955, the Senate, led by Sen. Wright, chair of the Senate tax committee, waited until near the end of the session and voted to kill withholding, even in the face of overwhelming public support. No budget crisis was pending in 1957, however—thanks largely to the reforms transferring iron-ore tax revenues as authorized by the constitutional amendment approved by voters in 1956. Freeman, like a seasoned general, chose not to engage the Senate over withholding. He could wait, so he declared victory. Minnesota's economy was growing, aid to education had increased, spending on state programs was higher, and Minnesota began to prepare for the centennial of its statehood in 1958.

Freeman did not have to wait long for a battle over withholding. While Minnesota celebrated its centennial, the national economy was heading south, leaving Minnesota to face a fiscal hangover of major proportions in 1959. Freeman capped the celebration in November by winning a third term as governor with the largest majority of his career—only to face the largest postwar budget deficit to date.

Top DFL leaders and legislators received the bad news on the 1960–61 budget in a private briefing on December 26 from Walter Heller, Freeman's tax advisor, and Joe Robertson, state tax commissioner, in the conference room of the Veterans Building on the capitol grounds. The approaching legislative session would have to figure out a way to raise as much as $90 million in new revenues, or 17 percent above current revenue projections, over the next biennium, Heller said. The report hit the participants like a bucket of cold water. The tax issue would dominate the 1959 legislature.[9]

After the presentation, Freeman rose to speak. He would ask for withholding and raise individual and corporate income-tax rates as well as iron-ore, royalty, and excise taxes. He wanted an increase in dependent credits for children and elderly to offset income-tax rates. He would allow increases only to maintain programs at the bare minimum. Freezing the salaries of state employees was a distinct possibility. Per-pupil aid must increase to $87 per year, as required by a reform package adopted by the 1957 legislature for education.

An hour-long discussion followed. Fred Cina, Aurora, who would be named House majority leader, and Don Wozniak, St. Paul, who would continue as chair of the House tax committee, said the House would support the governor. A voice said the Senate would be a different story, and no one disagreed.

The governor's January 14 budget message was the most widely anticipated political event of the year as the legislature opened its 61st session in 1959. The Conservatives had elected John Zwach, Walnut Grove, as Senate majority leader. Donald Wright, Minneapolis, retained his position as chair of the Senate tax committee. Zwach said, "I want as little politics and as much hard work as possible."

Freeman proposed to spend $483 million on state services over the next two years. He said anticipated revenues from current tax levels would raise about $388 million. An increase in taxes of $85 million was needed to balance the biennial budget. He proposed withholding, or pay-as-you-go, on individual income taxes. He suggested an increase of 1 percent for each income-tax bracket and a 1 percent increase in corporate income taxes. Iron-ore taxes also would increase, as would a variety of excise taxes. He said, once again, that he opposed a sales tax, but he did not mention a veto of a sales-tax bill.

He had pared down requests for agency budgets, allowing only the increases necessary to maintain public services. The education equalization fund adopted in the 1957 legislature had committed the state to spending $18 million more in 1959–60 than estimated in 1957. He did not propose changing the formula. His budget increased per-pupil state aid to $87 per student per school year. He noted that a 50 percent drop in anticipated iron-ore shipments during the recession of 1959 and 1960 was a major contributing factor to the deficit.

Although he proposed no new spending programs, Freeman set out a number of "good government" recommendations, almost all destined for the committee on civil administration, chaired by Gordon Rosenmeier, Little Falls. Freeman urged a reapportionment to reflect changes in Minnesota's population distribution over the preceding 45 years (the legislature had last been apportioned in 1914). He asked the legislature to authorize an electronic data-processing center to modernize Minnesota's record-keeping systems, noting its potential for substantial savings in administrative costs as well as improved government services. Freeman recommended that the legislature establish an atomic energy board to monitor state policies on nuclear safety and energy development. He proposed adoption of an ethics code for state government officials with a provision requiring all legislative lobbyists to register. He also asked the legislature to enact a proposal for government reorganization, pointing out that the plan would help taxpayers by improving services and reducing administrative costs.[10]

The reaction was surprisingly muted. Senate Majority Leader Zwach said he was sure the Senate "could find excess fat that can be cut without curtailing state services." Senate tax committee chair Wright said, "The budget is ambitious, expensive, and luxurious. The tax plan narrows the tax base and increases the rate, when we should broaden the tax base and decrease the rates."[11] The next day the *Minneapolis Tribune* published a table showing the increases of Freeman's tax proposal by income bracket—amount and percentage in each bracket.[12] A four-person household earning $50,000 a year would pay an additional $341 a year in income taxes, or an increase of 6 percent after deducting federal taxes A household earning $4,000 would pay $21 more or an increase of 75 percent. A household earning $12,000 would pay $85 more, or an increase of 16 percent.

Depicting the increase in percentage terms stung Freeman and the DFL. The governor appeared on a special TV program January 16 to defend his proposal and criticize the *Tribune* chart. The impact of a sales tax, compared to the income tax increase, he argued, would have been substantially greater for middle- and lower-income taxpayers. Freeman was correct, but he was caught in a dilemma of his own making. No legislator would propose a sales tax; offering a sales tax for comparison opened the door for a debate on the sales tax.

On the one hand, Freeman was setting the terms of the tax debate by proposing a balanced budget that relied on a relatively progressive income tax. On the other, no one was coming forward with a sales tax or a set of cuts in programs and services. Gerald Heaney, Democratic national committeeman and one of Freeman's close political advisors, at an all-day DFL teach-in on budgets and taxes on January 24 in Minneapolis, predicted the legislature would come within $4 million of granting the governor's spending request.[13]

The approaching crisis, like two trains headed for each other on the same track, was obvious. The legislature could not find any place to cut the state budget for programs and services without offending major voting blocs and program constituencies. Neither would any legislator—Liberal or Conservative—propose a sales tax as an alternative to the Freeman tax plan. While Freeman could define the playing field, the Senate Conservatives controlled the timing of the game. Freeman could do little to force the issue. All he and DFL legislators could do was wait. Senate Conservatives could afford to wait as well. Newly elected to four-year terms, the Conservatives believed voters would not remember in 1962 any crises they might have initiated in 1959. Eventually, they assumed, Freeman would have to offer a sales tax to close the deficit.

The Waiting Game: High-Risk Strategy

Playing the waiting game was a high-risk strategy for both the DFL and the Republicans. DFL members looked uneasily at the precedent of the 44-day special session called in 1937. Republicans took comfort from the outcome of legislative events 20 years earlier. Farmer-Labor Gov. Elmer Benson had called that special session to resolve a deadlock over an increase in taxes to close a deficit brought on by the economic slowdown in 1936. Elected by a record 250,000-vote margin in 1936, Benson watched his commanding political strength rapidly erode the following summer. The legislative session wore on, grinding away at the Farmer-Labor Party's eight-year dominance. The special session concluded in late June, as did the party's political future. In 1938 the Republican candidate, Dakota County Attorney Harold Stassen, defeated Benson by almost 300,000 votes. Republican candidates swept all state offices for the next 17 years.

Freeman had little choice but to accept the Conservatives' timing of the battle over taxes. He had been elected to govern, but he also had built a foundation for responsible governance that stood him good stead for the crisis. He launched a ten-day, 33-city speaking tour to build support around the state. He ran on a record of good government. As governor-elect in 1954 he had gone to Wall Street to plead for Minnesota as a state with potential for growth and investment. In 1955 he had first proposed withholding as a policy to close a hole in state tax statutes allowing tax cheats to evade paying almost $2 million a year. The loss, Freeman tirelessly explained to voters, came from the pocket of the honest taxpayers making up the difference.

Faced with an estimated deficit of $83.7 million in 1959, Freeman proposed following the tax-study recommendations. That meant relying on tax sources already in use—that is, increases in personal income taxes combined with withholding—as the primary source of new revenues. Increases in iron-ore taxes and selected excise taxes (a form of sales tax) would make up the difference.

The Governor's Tax Study Committee represented both a political initiative and a managerial objective for Freeman. He believed a bipartisan committee could help convince Republican (Conservative) legislators to support withholding. He succeeded in that goal but not in 1957 or 1959. Conservative legislators after the 1959 legislative session described the tax study report, as "THE thing to refer to . . . That was kind of the Bible [on tax policy]."[14] In 1959, however, the Senate studiously ignored the study. Contrary to majority leader Zwach's pledge of "hard work" by Conservative senators, the Senate sat on its hands through February and March, giving little attention to tax proposals.

The dispute between Freeman and the Senate Conservatives was a complex mixture of institutional rivalry and personal animosity. Governors then served two-year terms while senators were elected every four years.[15] The difference in length of terms was a disadvantage for the governor who might be unable to devote more than two years to a priority issue. This also affected the relationship between competing political institutions and the heads of state agencies, who in the 1950s held appointments that could survive the election or defeat of a sitting governor. Agency heads, however, always had to deal with state senators who served four-year terms. Karl Grittner, a St. Paul DFL Liberal in the Minnesota Senate during and for 20 years following Freeman's tenure, described the Senate relationship with governors as uneasy. "The Senate," Grittner said, "liked to have weak governors, and members of the Senate apparently liked to deal with departmental heads who are more responsible to them than to the governor."[16]

Freeman was not a weak governor. He chose in 1959 to drop the political gauntlet of withholding as the centerpiece of DFL tax policy, ensuring the longest special legislative session in Minnesota history. His efforts to defeat Senators Wright and Rosenmeier in 1958, a strategy to strengthen support for a progressive tax system, could not help but ensure that both Conservatives would bear strong, personal grudges. They would make Freeman's life as governor unbearable in 1959. But animosity toward Freeman also led the Conservatives to make a fatal judgment—that of allowing Senator Wright to wear the mantle of public champion for Conservatives and Republicans as to taxes and public services. Wright and the Senate Conservative majority rejected withholding. In so doing they had to propose spending programs without tax proposals. The irresponsible stance was the beginning of the Conservatives' decline as majority caucus; it seriously weakened the Minnesota Republican Party as a political force. In the end, confrontation with a strong-willed chief executive initiated a longer-term shift in the organization and function of the Senate. This led to the demise of a leadership system built around strong committee chairs and to the rise of the strong majority leader.

The confrontation began on April 24, the closing day of the 90-day legislative session. Both the House and the Senate had approved proposals for education, transportation, government operation, and health and welfare. These called for spending $483 million for the biennium. Conference committees held those bills pending action on a tax, or revenue, bill. On April 16 the House approved and sent to the Senate a tax bill, House File (HF) 1, an omnibus tax plan authorizing $483 million in revenues, including the sources for an increase of $83 million proposed in Freeman's budget message. Wright's committee, which had held hearings on taxes over the preceding three months, did not act immediately on the bill.

Wright introduced his tax plan on Tuesday, April 21. He proposed to strip withholding from the House bill, drop the 1 percent increases in individual- and business-income taxes, eliminate the 1 percent increase in iron-ore taxes, and drop the proposals for inheritance and gift taxes. Wright proposed to retain a one-cent increase on packages of cigarettes and to double to 10 percent the surtax on liquor. The tax committee voted to adopt the Wright proposal. The full Senate approved the tax committee report and returned the House bill, now shorn of the new revenue proposals. Liberal Sen. Donald Fraser, Minneapolis, pointed out that the Senate now had no appropriation bill. The tax committee's action had left the Senate about $107 million short of what it had earlier approved in spending.[17] The House rejected the Senate proposal and returned the original HF 1 tax proposal to the Senate.

Each legislative body appointed five members to a conference committee on taxes that met on April 22 and 23. Majority leader Fred Cina, a House conferee, said the House would not back away from its proposal to balance revenues with spending. Wright refused to submit a proposal that would enable the Senate to meet its constitutional obligations.[18] Rather than engage in last-minute negotiations as had occurred when Freeman and the DFL House leaders agreed to drop withholding in 1955, Freeman said he would call a special session to start April 25. Although a governor cannot dictate to the legislature the issues considered in a special session, both Liberal and Conservative leaders agreed they would deal with unfinished business—the legislation on taxes and appropriations then pending.

Cina said the House would meet on Monday, April 27, to reenact the House tax bill as the basis for negotiations in the conference committee on taxes. Zwach said the "Senate wants a recess to rest." The *Minneapolis Tribune* noted that the Senate was stalling on the issues of a computer system for electronic data processing, an atomic energy board, lobbying registration, and ethics in government.[19] The report, summarizing the status of legislation enacted by the House, also said that the Rosenmeier committee had rejected the government reorganization bill. The *Tribune* reported that a key reason cited by legislators for Senate opposition was that "the Senate does not want Freeman to campaign and take credit for the proposals." The *Sunday Star and Tribune* (April 26) compared the Senate to the House, "where action on all important legislation was completed." It noted that "the Senate has far to go." On Monday, April 27, the House met and adopted HR 1 as Cina had promised. The Senate met briefly to adjourn until Thursday, April 30, as Zwach had pledged.

Newspaper editors around Minnesota were not amused by the political antics in St. Paul. "This is probably the most futile and frustrating session we have had for many years," the *St. Cloud Times* editorialized, "We know something is mighty wrong and needs fixing." The *Park Region Echo* in Alexandria agreed:

The chief reason for the chaos in the legislature remains the Conservative Senate leadership's determination to block, stall, or mutilate any of the legislation asked for by Governor Freeman in welfare, education, government reform, and other important areas and its unwillingness or inability to submit programs of its own.

The *Brainerd Daily Dispatch* concluded that it was "apparent from the first that some sort of compromise would have to be reached in a tax program. Yet no effort has been made by either side." The *West*

Central Daily Times, Willmar, was more pointed: "If the Senate wants a sales tax so badly, they had better sell it to the people at the next election and try to get a House and a governor who are for it."

Apparently oblivious to the views from outstate Minnesota, the Senate returned on May 4 from its recess without offering any hint of compromise. The Senate killed legislation on lobbying registration, ethics in government, an atomic energy board, and government reorganization. Wright proposed that the Senate tax committee strip the new revenue provisions from the House bill, putting the Liberal tax increases in a separate bill. The committee then killed it. To underscore his determination to force Freeman and the Liberal House leadership to propose a sales tax, Wright offered as a revenue measure the shell of the House bill. Once again the Senate refused to propose a balanced budget, waiting for the governor to offer a compromise. A group of House Conservatives nervously started drafting an alternative tax proposal based on federal income taxes. While some Conservatives objected that an initiative by House Conservatives would embarrass Wright and the Senate, others defended the action as "moving in the right direction since the Senate hadn't proposed an alternative.[20]

On May 4, Monday, in response to an invitation from the governor, the House and Senate members of the tax conference committee met for 53 minutes in the ornate governor's office.[21] Freeman said he was flexible on withholding but would not withdraw the measure. He offered a plan to forgive the first six months of 1959 income taxes rather than the four months contemplated in his initial proposal. Then, for the first time publicly, he said he would veto a sales tax.

Wright emerged from the meeting furious and criticized the governor's "ultimatum." He apparently had expected Freeman to abandon withholding and request that the legislature enact a sales tax. He said the "ultimatum puts the burden of the tax increase on income taxpayers" and charged that "this extravagant and money-spending administration" had caused the financial crisis. Other Senate conferees said the "straitjacket veto threat has made impossible the Senate hope to protect the economic future of the state."

Freeman discussed in a public meeting the reason for his decision:

I would veto a sales tax because that is my obligation and responsibility to people who have elected me to office. I have clearly and consistently expressed opposition during all my years in public life . . . I have been elected with that position well known to those who elected me.

He reminded listeners that the Republican Party had rejected the sales tax at its convention in 1958.[22]

Although the outline for the tax compromise—reliance on individual and corporate income taxes as the primary source for new revenues—had emerged in the May 4 meeting, the special session dragged on over withholding another eight weeks. Wright unalterably opposed it, and the House DFL majority, angered by the behavior of Senate Conservatives, now was willing to go to the mat.[23]

On May 15 the Senate rejected the House Liberal proposal to revive pay-as-you go, offering instead a tax plan based on individual and corporate income taxes, to raise $53 million of the $86.5 million gap. The Senate offered to include authority to borrow from the income-tax school fund to cover the possible deficit. The tax conference committee could not agree on the Senate proposal.

The Senate conferees rejected a May 22 proposal by Freeman to forgive 100 percent of the withholding windfall and install withholding on July 1, 1959. Personal income taxes due before July 1959 would be canceled. Wright rejected the compromise plan. Tempers were raw. On May 25 Cina accused Senate Conservatives of causing the impasse: "When the Senate found that Freeman would veto a sales tax, [it] had to start all over and lay out a plan without withholding because [it] had no other plan."

The Senate conferees rejected on May 26 a proposal of the House conferees to put withholding to a vote in the 1960 election. Wright dismissed the offer as a "political move." Sen. Fay George Child, Clara City, complained on the Senate floor that Lt. Gov. Karl Rolvaag in a Minneapolis speech had called Conservative Senators "tired old men with a total lack of responsibility." He asked Rolvaag not to "forget the dignity of your position."

Rolvaag, asking to reply as a matter of personal privilege, retorted, "I spoke on the difference in philosophy of my party and your party." Majority leader Zwach rose on May 27 to warn Conservatives that the Minnesota Farmers Union was sending busloads of farmers to the capitol to call for withholding. "This is extreme pressure," he complained.[24]

The standoff continued. Wozniak, chair of the House tax committee, told Wright on May 28, "I will quit [the conference committee] if you will quit." Wright snorted, "I never quit a fight."

The conferees agreed on May 31 to ask their respective caucuses to send new conferees to the conference committee. The House waited for the Senate to announce its new delegation before appointing its own conferees. Wright and Zwach led the new Senate conferees. Wozniak and Cina continued to lead the House conferees. The *Minneapolis Tribune* reported on June 4 that the first meeting of the new conference committee "came up with familiar, well-worn statements."

With the political storm engulfing the legislature, Freeman had quietly developed an exit strategy in early May.[25] He asked Heller to prepare a set of tax-policy alternatives for him and the House Liberal caucus to evaluate. Freeman's political options narrowed during the legislative session. He had sought to rally public support for programs and for withholding, but Senator Wright, angered by political pressure, was oblivious to public opinion. Even as public support for the Conservative position slipped away, Republicans made no move to distance themselves from Wright.[26] The Governor's Tax Study Committee had achieved critical academic and public acclaim, but business leaders remained aloof from the crisis, providing no support. "I am at a loss to know what to do next," Freeman wrote to Heller.

On May 29 Heller prepared a confidential memo examining five options—"Methods of Breaking the Tax Deadlock."[27] Freeman circulated the memo for discussion by a handful of trusted advisors and key legislative leaders:

- Position I: Hold tight to the July 1, 1959, withholding and the proposed rate increases. Increase forgiveness to the 1943 federal approach—forgive three-quarters of 1958 or 1959 liabilities, whichever was lower. This would require tax-anticipation borrowing of $18.5 million against the withheld tax for April through June 1961.
- Position II: Wright had indicated on public television's Channel 2 that his minimum price for withholding was some "third form" of tax, that the suggestion of a $5 minimum tax was worth exploring, and that the search might be for something to save face for Wright without bending liberal principles. A $5 minimum tax might be a reasonable price to pay for July 1, 1959, withholding.
- Position III: Postponement of withholding.
- Position IV: A November 1960 referendum on withholding suggested putting the proposed tax rates into effect July 1, 1959, so that only half the impact would hit in 1960. Taxpayer payments would amount to $87 million for fiscal year 1959 and $103 million in fiscal 1960. With tax-anticipated borrowing of $18 million against withholding payments, this provide revenues of $208 million from individual income taxes for the biennium—the amount requested in Freeman's January tax proposal.

- Position V: Give in on withholding. Hold tight to the rest of the tax proposal. Use July 1, 1959, as the effective date for individual income-tax increases, as in Position IV (that is, with no retroactive increase). In light of the required appropriation cuts and the fast economic recovery, the option would yield enough revenue.

Wright and the Senate Conservative conferees rejected all House proposals based on the Heller options, including the 1960 referendum on withholding. Freeman sought other options, including a Minnesota variation of the Washington State business and occupations tax, a tax on the privilege of engaging in business activities in the state.[28] The occupations tax would raise an additional $66 million, more than enough when combined with individual and corporate income taxes to cover the deficit and help reduce property taxes.

By June 10, Freeman and the House Liberals, aware that Wright and the Conservatives were still maneuvering on a sales tax, had begun to focus on another exit strategy. They would develop a proposal with two options, one with withholding and the other without.[29]

Should Wright and the Senate Conservatives reject both options and propose to discharge the conference committee (so as to force Freeman and the DFL to offer a sales tax to end the standoff), Fred Cina would refuse to discharge the conference committee. He would simply refuse to allow the Senate conferees to leave.[30] He would publicly charge Wright and the Senate Conservatives with attempting to create a crisis in state government.

With the end of the fiscal year (June 30) drawing near, Cina planned to announce that a continued tax stalemate would force the halt of state government. Rejection of the House tax proposal would characterize Wright and the Senate as attempting to force the governor to propose a sales tax. The state had permanent taxing authority to raise enough funds to finance its government for another three or four months, as both Cina and Wright knew. But with patience running thin among voters, Cina's charges would break the deadlock by placing the Senate at a disadvantage. Since Wright would propose no sales tax, the Senate could do nothing but accept the House options as a basis for final negotiation.

If the Senate rejected withholding, as everyone expected Wright to do, the Senate Conservatives could only take the second option, without withholding, as the basis for resolving the deadlock. If the Liberals did not get withholding, they could force the Senate Conservatives to accept a tax package shifting much of the burden to business and the iron-ore industry.

As Liberal leaders and Freeman's tax advisors reviewed and refined these ideas, the *Sunday Minneapolis Star and Tribune* reminded both sides that public sentiment was turning against further delay.[31] In an editorial-page article on June 22, the newspaper cynically depicted a typical week at the special session:

On Monday the conferees give optimistic interviews on progress. Tuesday, the Senate repeats it is firm against withholding. Wednesday, the conferees explore new revenue sources. Freeman and the Senate trade insults on Thursday. And, Friday the conferees reach another stalemate.

On June 23, after a tumultuous argument among Liberals, the House voted 88 to 42, with 58 Conservatives joining 30 Liberals, to propose a tax plan with the option to drop withholding. A majority of Liberals refused to give up on withholding. On Tuesday, House conferees offered Senate conferees a plan with two options. Under the first, withholding would start October 1, 1959, with the individual income-tax rate increased 0.4 percent effective July 1. Three-fourths of 1959 or 1960 personal income taxes, whichever was smaller, would be canceled. Corporate tax rates would increase 9.3 percent without federal deduction, effectively shifting half the payment of business taxes on income to the federal government. Excise taxes would increase; iron-ore occupation rates would increase significantly. A business and occupations tax would replace personal property taxes.

The second option would drop withholding. Personal income-tax rates would increase 0.5 percent retroactive to January 1, 1959. The corporate rate would increase to 9.5 percent with no federal deductibility. Excise taxes would increase, and iron-ore levies would rise significantly. The second option would ensure $87 yearly in per-pupil basic aid for education. Counties would be authorized to repeal personal property on household goods.

The Senate Conservatives accepted the second option with "modifications." The Senate rejected the corporate tax rates and the proposed levies on iron ore. Cina, now in the driver's seat, rejected the Senate proposals. "We have given up on withholding, and the House is in no mood to go further," he said.[32]

Cina's move to wrest the initiative on taxes from Wright and the Senate was a major factor in breaking the deadlock. But a more significant development contributed to the momentum. As the special session droned on, the Minnesota Tax Department (MTD) continued receiving new data on tax revenues. The iron-ore industry, looking nervously at the pending tax changes, substantially increased its estimates of iron-ore shipment during the next biennium. At present rates, the companies told the MTD, anticipated revenues from iron-ore shipments would produce an additional $11.2 million in the biennium. In addition, the 1959 economic recovery was moving faster by June than anticipated in December 1958. The MTD told Freeman and the tax conferees on that June 18 weekend that it anticipated the collection of almost $16 million more in personal and corporate income taxes. These and other changes in revenue estimates and spending assumptions reduced the $89 million deficit for the 1959–60 biennium by nearly half, to $46.6 million.[33]

On Friday, June 26, the tax conferees reached agreement on a biennial tax bill to be introduced the following Monday. Senate Majority Leader Zwach, however, asked that action be postponed for one day. "The Senate needs a good night's sleep," he explained.[34] The real reason was that Zwach had lost control of the Senate and needed a day to reassert his authority. Senator Rosenmeier was holding up agreement on the state building program over how much to spend on the Brainerd State Hospital.

On Tuesday, June 30, the last day of the fiscal year, both houses passed the omnibus tax bill. Freeman immediately signed it into law. The legislation called for an increase in tax revenues of $47 million. Individual income taxes increased 0.5 percent, corporate income taxes 2 percent, cigarette taxes 1.5 cents a pack. Liquor and beer taxes increased, as did iron-ore taxes. Cina told the House that withholding would have allowed the legislature to eliminate increases on cigarettes and beer, corporate income, and iron ore. Wright opposed the bill in a "thundering" tirade because the beer tax was included without hearings.[35] Only four Conservatives joined him in opposition.

The special session did not end until July 1, the next day. The conferees on the state building program bill had agreed to include $4 million to begin a $13-million building at the Brainerd State Hospital. Rosenmeier, chair of the Senate committee on civil administration with jurisdiction of the legislation, wanted to spend the full $13 million. House members, exhausted and angry over Rosenmeier's part in killing the major "good government" bills passed by the House, threatened to cut the entire building program unless Rosenmeier accepted the $4-million appropriation. Since this also would have cut U of M authorization to begin building its West Bank campus, university supporters mobilized to put pressure on Rosenmeier, who relented, protesting that the House Liberals were punishing him.[36]

Editorial writers, calling the 1959 legislative session the "longest, most political in the history of the state," described the tax program as "a product of legislative exhaustion" and lamented the Conservatives' determination to give Freeman "nothing on which to campaign in 1960."[37] As Heaney had predicted six months earlier, the legislature gave Freeman the budget he requested, appropriating $487.7 million of the $488.5 million Freeman had proposed, a difference of $791,790. The legislature also reapportioned its legislative districts for the first time in 46 years, resolved the rural-urban split over daylight saving time, gave a modest increase in salary to state employees, and adopted an integrated juvenile code.

Freeman said at the adjournment of the 1959 session:

Taxation is an important and integral part of our task—a part inseparable from the . . . goals we wish to reach, the programs our people need, and the vision we seek to realize.

Defects in our handling of tax problems inevitably affect our progress toward those goals. Inadequacies in our solution to the tax question are reflected in delayed action in building junior colleges where most needed, a slowing in progress toward improved mental-health facilities, and postponement of a more vigorous program to promote new business in our state.

The compromise tax bill that you have passed does not meet the standards I had hoped for. It includes more tax increases on both individuals and business than would have been necessary if the Senate had been willing to accept withholding. The tax program thus enacted includes some improvements in our tax structure. But it leaves many more improvements—such as property tax reform and pay-as-you-go collection of income taxes—for the future. I shall continue to work for those reforms, hopeful that a better political climate and further education and understanding will [ensure] their achievement.[38]

Governor Freeman made clear in his campaign materials the programs and policies he favored.

—7—

Programs & Policies

Governor Freeman, alone in Kandyohi County in the midst of his biennial "Report to Minnesota" speaking tour in December 1959, ordered the National Guard to close Wilson and Company's meatpacking plant in Albert Lea. The decision, made quickly, shocked almost every editorial writer in America, most of his peers in domestic governance, the nation's business elite, and many other citizens comfortable with the conventional wisdom of 1959.[1] The action put him on a collision course with the federal courts.

But calling out the National Guard to halt the production of a company whose management had precipitated a labor dispute spiraling rapidly towards violence was not a judgment of the moment. The decision was predictably consistent with Freeman's core beliefs. Groomed by experiences testing those beliefs—growing up in south Minneapolis as the Great Depression began, debating social policy at the University of Minnesota during hard times, maturing as a U.S. Marine under fire in the South Pacific, and hammering together the postwar DFL—he had confidently taken charge as the governor of Minnesota.

Freeman trusted his abilities and judgment. He had begun his political career at barely 30 years of age, driving alone on the campaign trail from town to town. His car had an outside loudspeaker to announce (amid the squawks of a reluctant sound system) his arrival on Main Street. Sometimes this Don Quixote of politics attracted an audience of only five or six, and he hated campaigning with a minuscule budget.[2] But where the personal commitment of others sometimes withered, Freeman showed, in his repeated willingness to return to the quest, that he valued direct contact with voters. His belief in education and hard work was grounded in strong family values. He had a natural instinct for leadership that drew in others and belied his sometimes studious behavior. On the football field he had grasped quickly the strength of teamwork. Combat had taught him that loyalty and trust are the glue of organizational achievement. Freeman knew his own strength and exercised it with a pragmatic enthusiasm, sometimes mistaken for aggression, that led others to believe in shared goals.

Freeman's acquaintance with death in the jungles of Bougainville Island gave him the innocence free of arrogance to say he had not come home to be a plumber. He attached little importance to fitting in. He believed government could be a positive force in the lives of people and communities. He held strong beliefs and was quick to respond to criticism.[3] He spoke directly to any subject with candor and without embarrassment, and he practiced what he preached.

As the 1954 campaign for governor drew to a close, for example, Freeman told a student convocation at Gustavus Adolphus College on October 29 that he viewed American democracy as balancing on three bedrock beliefs. First, he said, speaking as a Lutheran:

the church . . . is vital not only to our spiritual needs but also to community needs . . . The second is home and family, fundamental values that, only if lived day by day, will insure our nation continues strong and virile in the tradition of Christian freedom. The third is active participation as a voter, party worker and, yes, as a candidate in our democratic political process.

We are faced with a worldwide struggle in which leadership is thrust upon us, a time when we ourselves are struggling to define exactly how these basic moral principles fit in as a practical matter in our industrial society. In my humble judgment there is no area of human experience where more can be done to serve God and help other people than in public life.

Speaking on the eve of the election from which the DFL would emerge to dominate Minnesota politics for the next 40 years, Freeman described the contrasting political philosophies of the two contending parties:

The basic difference of approach between the Republican and Democratic parties today rests in the question of how much government should act in the realm of our economic life. I believe in a positive philosophy of government, with the responsibility resting in government [to use] its greater capital accumulation for natural resource development and to stimulate a constantly expanding and productive economy.

The Republicans, on the other hand, believe that government should play almost no part at all in the economic life of our nation. They are against public power and regional valley development based on an integrated approach to the problems of irrigation, navigation, flood control, and water. They opposed and fought the rural electrification program.

Freeman pragmatically described politics in the context of a fundamental tenant of Christian faith, holding that individual freedom is a gift of God that cannot be restrained or limited by governments or by other persons or institutions. Individual freedom exercised without restraint, however, could be a destructive force. Martin Luther spoke to that issue in reminding Lutherans of the advice in Luke 20:25 to render unto Caesar that which is Caesar's and unto God that which is God's. In the context of modern democracy, individuals may agree to extend certain rights essential for civil order, peace, and the common welfare to government, while retaining all other rights defining the relationship between themselves and their God. For instance, harnessing natural resources and controlling pollution of air and water—common resources—are tasks a complex society can undertake only when voters authorize their governments to accomplish those goals.

Freeman argued that in a complex world—such as the postwar industrial society of the 1950s—democratic governance has the potential to enhance the lives of people far beyond the capacity of individuals, each of whom has only limited authority and resources. In contrast, he said, Republicans believed American voters had already agreed to restrict individual freedom far more than necessary to create economic opportunity. And, he said, Republican voters should oppose doing more.

As mentioned in chapter 2, when returning home from the Gustavus Adolphus convocation in 1954, Freeman had been jolted from his philosophical exploration of the religious roots of political differences between Republicans and Democrats when he saw a Republican broadside stuck beneath the windshield wiper of an automobile parked near a roadside gas station. The missive charged that the Democrats constituted a war party, specifically responsible for World War II. The scurrilous propaganda sheet showed dead Marines floating in the surf of the Tarawa Island invasion. The piece was a brutal contrast to Freeman's statement of politics as a religious calling, and it reminded him that politics is also a contact sport. Considering its timing, Freeman's outrage at the handout likely reflected as much his recognition that fairness in politics is a non sequitur as it did the anger of a U.S. Marine veteran that the GOP was exploiting his dead comrades. He forcefully expressed that view in a television program two days later.

While few of the students attending the convocation likely were of voting age (21 at the time), six days later enough Minnesotans shared Freeman's philosophy to elect him the state's 29th governor. Upon his election in 1954, Freeman's task shifted. He now had to confirm as sound judgment the trust extended by the voters in selecting a DFL administration. His success in governing, as well as the political future of the party, required that the governor act as the party leader. Although his title did not include it, Governor Freeman grasped the political reality intuitively and the party leadership with enthusiasm.

In the 60 hectic days leading to his January 1955 inauguration, Freeman's meager staff worked full tilt.[4] The budget message, the single most important setting forth of the specifics of the first DFL program for Minnesota, was as yet unwritten. Freeman recalled his awareness of putting together an official statement that would show like no other the significance of the election—new government priorities presented in terms of dollars and cents.[5]

On January 19, 1955, the new governor told a joint session of the Minnesota Senate and the House of Representatives:

Our total financial resources are strong enough to enable us to progress towards higher standards of service in education, public welfare, mental health, agriculture, conservation, and highways—to mention only a few major areas. We, as a people, have the wealth to support these services; our problem is that we have not yet wholly convinced ourselves that government services, like private services, cost money, and that, if wisely conceived and properly administered, such services elevate our standard of living and actually improve our general financial situation.

Freeman said the state was facing a deficit of nearly $50 million with a budget of $337 million for the 1955–56 biennium. This would necessitate an increase in revenues of nearly 15 percent. While the figures seem almost negligible in comparison to the budget deficit of $4.5 billion for 2004–05, the deficits, though some 40 years apart, are roughly the same in proportion to total spending for each biennial period.[6] In 1955, an economic recession had lowered demand for iron ore and reduced the depletion-tax receipts, then a significant source of state revenue, especially for education. The recession also resulted in reduced revenues for railroads and their payment of a gross-earnings tax to the Minnesota general fund. The combined loss of revenues accounted for $5.7 million, more than 11 percent of the deficit.

The Minnesota budget relies on two funding channels for current expenses—the general revenue fund and the income-tax school fund—which must contain sufficient revenues to balance government expenditures. The Minnesota constitution prohibits deficit spending, that is, borrowing against future revenues to balance the budget. The state can borrow funds but only for capital expenditures to finance construction of new buildings and facilities. Excise taxes (mostly on cigarettes and beer), limited revenues from iron-ore taxes, revenue from railroads, and taxes on inheritance and gifts provide general revenue to support all state services other than public education. Revenues from the income-tax school fund plus investment income from trust funds supported by iron-ore-depletion taxes provide for a uniform per-pupil allocation to public schools. Education, including spending for public schools combined with other educational programs (primarily the University of Minnesota), for what is now MNSCU, and for junior colleges, is by far the single largest and most important public service financed by Minnesota taxpayers.

After personally reviewing budget requests from the departments providing services to Minnesota citizens, Freeman proposed to increase overall spending by agencies and departments by about 8 percent. This compared with departmental requests of nearly 14 percent. General revenue needs for operating state government would increase by $11 million over the 1954–55 biennium. Included in that amount was a $1.5 million increase in old-age assistance to a monthly maximum from $60 to $65 per person. At slightly more than 8 percent a month, it was to be the first such increase in more than a decade.

Increased taxes from three sources—mostly from higher rates on iron-ore shipments to provide $8 million in new revenues—made up more than half the deficit in the general revenue fund. "The evidence that iron ore can absorb a substantial increase in taxation," Freeman said, "is conclusive." Iron-ore tax rates in 1955 were lower than in the 1930s and roughly the same as in 1941, he explained. The rates provided about as much per ton of ore as Minnesota received in excise taxes on a carton of cigarettes.

Freeman said the increase in taxes on iron ore met his criteria—to spread the tax load broadly and fairly according to ability to pay and to maintain Minnesota's competitive position among neighboring states. In addition, he wished tax measures to be fairly and economically administered. He wished to continue preferential tax treatment for taconite as an investment in developing Minnesota's future.

The inheritance and gift tax represents one of the best examples of the ability-to-pay criterion, Freeman said, because it effectively differentiates those who do and those who do not enjoy inherited wealth. The higher rates would eventually raise an additional $2 million per year. He noted that the tax structure was to bear lightly on widows and children but more heavily on distant relatives.

Annuities, or premiums paid for retirement income, are a profitable source of income for insurance companies, Freeman said, as profitable as premiums paid for protection at death. Minnesota, like other states, taxed insurance premiums, but the state did not tax premiums on the sale of annuities as other states did. Bringing annuities into the insurance-tax base would raise $600,000 in new revenues yearly and help spread the tax load through a tax that insurance companies easily could pay.

Freeman did not ask for higher taxes on wine and liquor but did propose raising $2.1 million a year on excise taxes on beer, an increase of less that one-fifth of one cent per bottle. He said wine and liquor taxes in Minnesota were among the nation's highest, while the tax on beer was among the lowest. This policy would spread the tax load more broadly and fairly. Since Minnesota then had far more beer drinkers than wine connoisseurs, the increase per bottle was minimal. He proposed an increase in taxes on tobacco but not on cigarettes. Minnesota had a four-cent tax per pack on cigarettes, higher than that of most other states, but it did not tax other tobacco products. Freeman wished to place a 20 percent tax on the retail price of all tobacco products, to raise $2 million for the biennium.

Turning to a $20 million deficit in the income-tax school fund, Freeman said the problem would become even more serious; the deficit represented only a trickle of the approaching tidal wave of education costs for postwar baby boomers. The school-age population would increase by more than 50,000 children in the next biennium:

> This factor alone will place a tremendously increased burden upon the school fund, [and] a vastly increased demand for teachers and buildings. [S]chool districts must have still larger state assistance if we are to maintain present standards, which are by no means extravagant.

Raising those revenues would require major reforms in funding and tax policy. The state was paying $80 per pupil in aid to school districts, which would cost Minnesota $158 million for the biennium without approved increases. But "to stand still at $80 per pupil state aid is to allow our educational system to slip back," Freeman said. "There is no escaping the necessity of providing a substantial increase in basic aid. I am on record and wish to restate my position that I favor increasing the basic aid from $80 to $92 per student."

This proposal would increase the budget deficit by about $20 million for the biennium without raising income-tax rates. Freeman did not stop there, instead proposing an overall increase in income-tax revenues of $30 million to include a modest increase in income-tax deductions for dependents as well to put $6 million in a carryover fund for use in the event of falling income-tax revenue. The carefully devised proposal was a reform measure meant to achieve three policy objectives:

1. provide a significant increase in state aid to public schools
2. hold personal income-tax rates at current levels
3. block a general sales tax, a regressive revenue measure falling hardest on those least able to pay.

The problem was that reform would take at least four years. The long-term goal was to direct iron-ore tax revenues into current education spending. Under the state's constitution, most revenues for iron-ore taxes were deposited in trust funds. Only the investment earnings from these funds could go towards education. With all iron-ore revenues available for current use, the income-tax school fund would receive as much as an additional $22.4 million each biennium and the University of Minnesota would receive up to an additional $5.6 million. While the shift would largely eliminate the 1955 budget, voters first must amend the constitution. That couldn't happen until the next general election in 1956.

If the deployment of iron-ore revenues to current expenditures for education could not close the deficit in 1955, then at least the deficit would not occur in 1957. The problem was to find $23 million for the income-tax school fund over the next two years without raising rates. Freeman and his tax advisors had a neat solution: Withhold personal income taxes—the pay-as-you-go plan the federal government had adopted in the early days of World War II—to collect taxes on wages and earnings. In 1954 nearly all Minnesota taxpayers paid income taxes in one lump sum, on March 15 every year. Some saved to meet the payment, but the obligation hovered like a specter over most wage earners, disrupting family budgets.

Withholding had many positive features. For taxpayers living from paycheck to paycheck, the March 15 crunch of a lump-sum payment would vanish. The absence of an overhanging tax liability would substantially ease payment. Cheating would also disappear. Some citizens never paid their income-tax obligations, and enforcement was difficult because information on income was not easily available. Withholding would substantially reduce, if not eliminate, a practice that cost Minnesota an estimated $2 million in lost tax revenues each biennium. In effect, other taxpayers made up the lost revenues.

Withholding was essential to Freeman's tax-reform measure. The state would collect in two years the payment of personal income-tax obligations for three years.[7] Payments would double temporarily through a shift in tax payments to a current basis. In effect, the state would borrow the money at a time when most taxpayers experienced peak earnings and were likely to handle the payment more easily. It would forgo collecting taxes when payment was more difficult.

In exchange for withholding, Freeman proposed to hold personal-income-tax rates steady and extended an implied promise that the state could, for at least the next four years, meet the growing demand for educational funding without raising its rates. His reform measure offered insightful economic policy essential for a state that depended increasingly on personal wealth created through innovation rather than exploitation of natural resources (iron ore, timber, and agriculture). Rather than pile iron-ore revenues into funds that would erode in value through inflation over the rest of the 20th century, the state would invest the cash flow from depletion of Minnesota resources in research, development, and a highly educated workforce. Personal incomes would grow faster, with more people employed in higher income jobs than in low-skill work. Tax revenue from incomes would grow faster to support an education system capable of responding to the changing needs of Minnesota residents. Freeman's tax-reform policy would shift the tax system from a shrinking revenue stream to a sustainable revenue stream based on the constantly expanding, renewable economy of human creativity that education makes possible.

Withholding was a critical element in the future of a state financial system based on income growth to fund a spending program in which public education received the largest single share of revenues for services. Long-term support for education depended on an income-tax system capable of producing significant revenues that depended in turn on a system of tax collection enabling citizens to more easily meet their tax obligations.

While Republicans in the 1955 state legislature supported education (and social services, less enthusiastically), both they and most Minnesota newspapers wanted a sales tax. They had sought every opportunity to enact a sales-tax measure but did not have the political power to enact one over a governor's veto. The only strategy available was to use a budget crisis like the one that came along that year. Here was an opportunity the GOP was not about to forgo. Neither would it consider withholding, especially if it might complicate the GOP strategy for enactment of a general sales tax.

In retrospect, the GOP strategy on withholding was self-defeating and politically shortsighted. The legislature adopted the proposal to submit to voters a constitutional amendment to permit use of iron-ore taxes for current budget needs. The Minnesota Senate, overwhelmingly dominated by Republicans, rejected the tax recommendations proposed by Freeman and the DFL. The effect was to create a short-term crisis as a pretext for adoption of a sales tax. Had the GOP embraced withholding in 1955, the opposition of Freeman and the DFL to the sales tax in the 1959 legislature (national recession had led to another budget crisis) would have been less credible.

The 1955 DFL strategy focused on long-term goals reflecting the views of a majority of Minnesota voters. Withholding and a general sales tax competed to address the 1955 budget crisis, but neither won that year. The opposition of the GOP to a tax policy proposing neither higher income-tax rates nor a general sales tax, however, gave high ground to the DFL in a debate repeated almost every two years for the rest of the century. Freeman had six years' advantage to build public momentum for the support of a progressive tax policy to finance a liberal program of social services, especially education.

The 1955 budget proposal was a message to Minnesotans in the value of building their state and its capacity to grow. Freeman's budget recommendations included substantial increases in the building program for state schools, colleges, hospitals, the University of Minnesota, and other facilities, including state parks and recreation areas. In comparison, the preliminary budget drafted by outgoing Gov. C. Elmer Anderson had included a spending proposal for new construction and maintenance of state facilities less than necessary even for adequate maintenance.[8] In another demonstration of innovative tax policy, Freeman proposed to spend $29.4 million for new construction and maintenance, a package that would double to $58.5 million the state's indebtedness, to finance state building programs while reducing property-tax rates. Noting that 15-year bonds financed current debt, Freeman said, "I see no reason why this entire amount could not be spread over a 20-year amortization base, which would . . . actually be a modest bit of tax relief for property owners."

Freeman deplored the lack of attention by past administrations and the legislature to deteriorating state hospitals, schools, and other facilities. He pointed out that some buildings had been in use for more than 75 years while others were so obsolete and unsafe as to put the lives of patients and employees in jeopardy. New buildings could help consolidate dispersed employees in some departments at less cost than the annual rentals for space. Construction of new classrooms and research facilities at the University of Minnesota, in the state universities, and at junior colleges was critical to meeting the coming demand for higher education.

The message jolted the legislature into action. "We should put an end to the haphazard and unsystematic manner in which we have handled our building problems," Freeman said. His proposal for a permanent building commission to recommend a long-term building plan updated every two years and with authority to approve specific building projects failed approval. But the legislature did approve a joint House-Senate building committee to meet when the legislature was not in session. In the committee's first two years of investigations, the commissioner of administration, appointed as chair, had the power to break ties in the vote. Led by Commissioner Art Naftalin, the committee spent 1955 and 1956 examining the state's building needs. In 1957 it recommended a $50 million building program including substantial expansion of the University of Minnesota campus, doubling again the indebtedness for state building projects. Naftalin continued as chair of the joint committee, though the legislators thoughtfully removed his authority to cast tie-breaking votes. They reasoned that only those persons elected to the legislature should have the privilege of a vote.

Perhaps with a premonition of approaching conflict, Freeman acknowledged the disadvantages that Minnesota had to overcome in creating a social framework that could foster economic growth. He discussed frankly the central role of tax policy in achieving those objectives. "We are far from mass markets, which means transportation is a heavy cost item on products sold outside of our natural trading area. Our climate is not favorable to many kinds of manufacturing, and our power costs are high compared to many parts of the country," he said.

Warning that criticism of the Minnesota tax structure as hostile to economic development is self-defeating, Freeman said:

> The time is overdue for everyone dependent on our state's economy—labor, management, farmers, cooperatives, the professions—to join in an honest and realistic appraisal of our assets and liabilities.
>
> We must face the economic facts of life. Our task is to determine our competitive position and the effects that each particular tax has upon our economy. When the facts show clearly that a tax is harmful to our economic position, we must courageously face up to our responsibility and make the necessary modifications.

Although Freeman invited the legislature to reduce the personal-property tax on manufacturers' tools and equipment and inventories, He was looking to a major policy initiative to revise Minnesota's tax structure and system.

After discussions with leaders in the business community, labor union officials, and farm organization leaders that began during the 1955 legislative session, Freeman announced on July 15, 1955, the creation of the Governor's Minnesota Tax Study Committee.[9] J. Cameron Thomson, chair of the board of Northwestern Bancorporation, agreed to chair the group and helped to raise $60,000 of the study's $70,000 cost from the business community. Unions and farm organizations provided the remaining funds. During preliminary discussions someone apparently decided to keep the committee wholly nonpartisan. No Minnesota legislators joined the businessmen, union officials, and farm organization leaders. Freeman noted in announcing the committee that he would have no official relationship with it.

Freeman's tax advisor, Walter Heller, was one of the committee's two academic members, however. His handprints are evidence of the role he played in the strategy enabling the committee to reach a successful conclusion. The committee began its work on November 5, 1955, and issued its recommendations on December 27, 1956.

The committee did not state a preference for personal income taxes or a general sales tax. It did warn policymakers of the central policy question that would confront every succeeding session of the Minnesota Legislature. The report stated:

> The time is near at hand in this state when the legislature must grant local communities authority to levy new nonproperty taxes of substantial revenue potential, or local government will have to appeal to the legislature for further and substantial grants-in-aid, or for further sharing of state-collected taxes, or both.

The committee did not propose new revenue sources to provide for those needs, opting instead for a delicately fashioned compromise treating the selection of a tax instrument as a technical issue. This allowed the committee's staff to recommend that policymakers consider a sales tax, a value-added tax, and a tax on personal income. The staff made a dispassionate case for structuring a system of credits to ensure that the sales tax would be progressive at low and middle incomes and proportionate in higher incomes. But it indicated no preference between a tax on purchases and one based on income.

The timing of the committee report gave Freeman the opportunity to propose withholding as a nonpartisan recommendation to the 1957 legislature, a failure in short-term budget strategy underscoring the reality that tax system changes usually occur during budget crisis. In 1957, with voter approval in 1956 to amend the constitutional provision on iron-ore taxes, the infusion of iron-ore tax payments directly into education-program funding, in addition to the recovery in employment as the 1955 recession ended, gave legislators a welcome respite from tax pressures. A fight over withholding was not to be. By 1957, however, when the Minnesota Senate again rejected withholding, GOP views on tax policy had begun to diverge significantly from those of the state's voters (more than 60 percent told pollsters they approved withholding). By 1960 even Elmer L. Andersen, the GOP candidate for governor, said he would veto a sales tax. The legislature enacted withholding in 1961 as a prudent budget measure.

The report had changed the political climate on tax issues, an important policy objective for Freeman. Voters now recognized the DFL as the party supporting a responsible debate on tax policy. Members of the party could associate their political views with a widely praised, nonpartisan examination of future revenue needs linking social programs, especially education, to the growth of the state's economy. Sales-tax advocates suddenly were on the defensive, no longer able to pose a sales tax as an alternative to income taxes. Instead they had to argue a that a regressive tax had desirable features not in evidence.

Freeman provided new status for the DFL while demonstrating the capacity to fashion a consensus among disparate centers of political interest on tax policy. He had isolated the political opposition in a nonpolitical context while achieving clear political objectives. The Office of the Governor had become a center of information and policy guidance on issues of governance. Freeman as party leader was educating key constituencies—academics, the voting public, government institutions, nongovernment institutions, the press, and party activists—in the philosophy that government can be a positive force in the lives of citizens.

Freeman made use of every possible opportunity to drive home the message of pragmatic liberalism. He generated a heavy speaking schedule, studies and reports, special legislative messages, press conferences, and weekly newspaper columns, especially in small towns.

On July 18, 1957, Freeman focused on health care at the dedication of a Community Health Center clinic in Two Harbors, Minne-

sota, a project of the Group Health Institute of the Cooperative
Health Federation of America. He praised the pioneering health-
maintenance program. Noting that community health service had its
start in Minnesota in 1946 at Two Harbors, he said group-health
practices required voluntary action, cooperation, community participation, and the principles of democratic action:

> In bringing to Minnesota its first plan for complete medical
> care on a prepayment basis, Two Harbors has struggled
> against the kind of resistance and inertia that always serves as
> bulwarks of the status quo. This courage to lead the way in the
> face of long-established methods that no longer serve their
> purpose is an urgently needed spirit and attitude in our rapidly
> changing world.

Improvements in health care and disease prevention add years to
life as well as life to years, Freeman said, but increased benefits also
mean increased costs:

> The cost of medical care is increasing rapidly. Expenditures for
> physicians' services in the United States have more than
> doubled in the past ten years. They are worth these increased
> costs. They hit hard, and unexpectedly, and without regard for
> the ability to pay.

Only his unconscious gender bias in assuming the head of the
family was male distinguishes Freeman's analysis of low income as a
barrier to health care from the state of health-care delivery today. He
cited studies finding that the bulk of expenditures by families for all
types of illnesses consisted of items not covered by health insurance.
Insurance benefits covered only 15 percent of total medical and hospital charges incurred by families.

"The value of this kind of protection should not be overlooked," Freeman said, noting that prepayment services, whether provided by health insurers or insurance companies, had increased significantly over the past decade:

> This constitutes genuine progress toward our goals, but it does not represent achievement of those goals. To collect from a major medical expense policy you must come close to the pearly gates. This is not health insurance. Health insurance should more adequately safeguard health and make available preventive care.

Voluntary prepayment plans offering really complete health care would require help if they were to expand fast enough and to enough people to meet real needs, Freeman said. He identified three key sectors where response was critical. "First, with adequate understanding and in a spirit of good will, doctors will extend their indispensable cooperation to any sincere program for extending the benefits of medical services to more people," he said. "Cooperation with prepayment health care plans will insure high standards and the control of professional services by professionally qualified personnel."

Second, organized labor and other economic organizations, particularly of farmers, would give impetus and encouragement to voluntary prepayment plans:

> In this field, labor, with its millions of members, has an opportunity to make a contribution of immeasurable value. It can choose between accepting provisions for ordinary kinds of sickness insurance or help organize and build plans that will provide complete health insurance. It can, through collective bargaining, provide its members with payments for such care

. . . Through education [it] can also further among its membership an understanding of the importance of preventive and complete care.

Third, Freeman cited government as crucial to the support of prepayment health plans. He noted that government provided incentives for public utilities, subsidies for publishers and advertisers using the postal service, subsidies to privately owned transportation firms and airlines and other profit-making enterprises. It did so on the basis that benefits would accrue to all citizens: "Voluntary, prepayment plans offering complete health care are of equal or greater importance to the public interest and should receive government support."

Freeman cited examples of support for health-care plans by the State of New York and the City of Philadelphia and noted that the federal government provided medical care directly in federal hospitals for veterans. Medical services for older indigent Americans was provided in Minnesota through the old-age-assistance programs where costs were increasing at more than 10 percent a year, doubling every six years.

Medical costs for older Americans, Freeman predicted, would continue to rise at a faster rate than for the population as a whole. He described the special irony of an aging population living longer and less dependent on public assistance because of Social Security but for whom retirement benefits were rarely enough to cover serious medical expenses.

Anticipating the major health-care reforms of a generation later, Freeman said:

I hope that we can explore the possibility of extending the voluntary prepaid medical care principle to a greater proportion of our aging citizens, especially for those over [age] 65. We should also consider whether to make it possible for other groups, such as those in lower income brackets, for whom voluntary programs seem too costly, to participate in such prepayment plans.

Easing tentatively into universal-health-care programs, he said:

We know there are millions of people whose incomes enable them to meet ordinary needs but are not large enough to cover the entire cost of participation in voluntary health-care plans. Others, during periods of unemployment, lose the group coverage they have. If we could devise an equitable and practical method by which government assistance would enable many of these families and individuals to participate in prepayment plans we might provide for better health care than they now receive.

In America we tend to decide whether or not government shall enter any field of enterprise on a realistic and pragmatic basis, and we do not ask government to provide services people need unless those services cannot or are not being provided by other means. We try, as I am suggesting here in the field of health care, to develop methods of government cooperation and assistance in working toward a socially desirable goal.

Freeman's informed examination of health-care policy offered specific remedies not only because he could obtain and organize specifics and document them but also because his chief policy advisor, Dorothy Jacobson, a national expert on health policy and group-health programs, drafted the speech. Because they shared political goals for more than a decade and worked on policy in the governor's office over three years, often in 15-hour days, their sense of detail, structure, content, and priorities by 1957 became almost the expression of a single mind.

Jacobson and Freeman also collaborated on a campaign using the governorship as a platform to build public support for raising the ethical standards for public officials and legislators in state government. Jacobson drafted a statement that Freeman used on September 22, 1957, to announce the appointment of a committee on ethics in government.[10]

The goal, Freeman said, was to eliminate or minimize the effect of self-interest on decision making, an issue that was less a matter of encouraging the better nature of public employees and elected officials than of discouraging the darker angel of human nature: "To the extent that prevailing practices and methods—rather than individual qualities—create or encourage such situations, a sincere effort to change such practices could materially improve standards of action."

The committee would not investigate specific lapses in judgment and integrity, Freeman explained, but would examine two areas—lobbying and conflicts of interest in both executive and legislative offices. It would recommend "steps forward in improving the principles and standards of government in Minnesota." He identified specific problem areas in lobbying, acknowledging that the activity fulfills an essential function by informing legislative and administrative action in complicated fields of public policy. Government, he said, involves weighing the arguments of one side in balance with the arguments on the other. But:

> The strength and effectiveness of a lobby may be all out of proportion to the numbers of people it represents. It may use methods of persuasion other than a presentation of the arguments. And it may even conceal its existence by failing to openly state what and whom it represents.

Conflicts of interest may present more stubborn problems than public disclosure could solve, Freeman said, noting that no legislator, administrator, or quasi-judicial or judicial official should act on a matter involving a direct financial interest. But he asked:

> How is the determination made as to the propriety of accepting a business luncheon or a weekend fishing invitation? When does a gift involve a courtesy and when does it become an obligation? These questions should be explored at length.
>
> What about legislators whose occupation may mean a conflict of interest in certain legislation? Many legislators represent trade associations, such as insurance council, savings-and loan-associations, bar associations, and various economic groups. Legislators are intimately involved with farm organizations in which they may own stock or hold office. Unions are represented in the legislature by employees, officers, and members. [W]here is the propriety when legislators are retained and paid fees by corporations, associations, private business and other interests?

Freeman said he was asking the ethics committee to recommend specific solutions, including legislation to prohibit lawyer legislators from representing private clients before any state agency whose actions might be influenced by their legislative status. The committee must consider legislation requiring public officials to disclose income-tax filings. Equally important, he said, was the committee's recommendation of a code of conduct for public officials describing specific examples of general propositions. A code of conduct would help public servants resist two frequent arguments in defense of questionable conduct—"everyone does it," and "it is part of the process." A code also would provide the public with clear criteria for measuring the conduct of public officials.

Minnesota legislators were in 1957 as unenthusiastic about disclosure of lobbying activities to improve confidence in government as they were 40 years later about proposals for a unicameral legislature. Nevertheless, public support resulted in adoption of a code of ethics for government officials and forced elected officials to portray in practice as well as to support a squeaky-clean image. In fact, Freeman was the first elected official to which the public applied his ethics yardstick—when he dismissed a former-aide-appointed-commissioner-of-insurance who breached the conflict-of-interest guidelines. The ethics issue reappeared when Freeman dismissed two other appointees for conflict-of-interest violations that some DFL officials believed were minor offenses. Some within the party criticized him for this action.

Both Freeman and Jacobson understood the role of education in building support for a pragmatic liberal program. And Freeman entrusted to Jacobson the broad responsibility for public information and education. No one wrote a strategic memo outlining such an objective or the assignment. Jacobson simply wrote speeches, reports, memos and statements, more than 300 columns, and the *Governor's Weekly Report* covering a wide range of program and policy matters. In fact, no better catalog of the educational goals of the Office of the Governor can be found than in a collection of *Weekly Reports* sent to Minnesota weekly newspapers. The columns are a unique political diary, a time capsule showing the ebb and flow of issues, the priorities, and the attention to detail that Minnesota's first DFL administration gave to the task of governance from January 2, 1955, through December 31, 1960.[11]

The weekly columns provided a set of policy arguments internally consistent with the liberal philosophy advanced by Freeman—that government could be a compassionate, positive force in the lives of individual citizens and families in Minnesota. The columns provided data and arguments on public schools, recreation, conservation, health policy, mental health, government services, higher education, the elderly, transportation, and public facilities—easily adaptable to public discussion in schools, civic clubs, churches, community organizations, women's groups, barbershops, morning coffee meetings, and carpools. The columns also served the management objective of informing state government departments and agencies of the priorities of the governor. This enabled Freeman to recognize public employees, that is to give programs and agencies highlighted in his column a pat on the back.

In January and February of 1957, for example, the weekly columns focused on the issues that the legislature was taking up. The January 22 column urged readers to examine the governor's budget message, warning that people would be "foolish to consider and evaluate the price he pays for a new car without considering the auto he is getting in return. The Tax Study Committee report is not the recommendations of the governor, although I endorse them, nor are they merely the program of a political party." Freeman promised that "if enacted, Minnesota will have the fairest and best tax program of any state."

The February 5 column summarizing Freeman's special message on education followed the discussion of tax policy. He asked the legislature for a five-dollar-per-pupil increase in state aid, warning that the cost of higher education was forcing deserving students to forgo college. He proposed a loan fund for qualified high-school graduates and advocated state assistance for junior-college students. On February 19 he turned attention to elderly citizens, describing the need for community programs including employment opportunities and recreational facilities, and recommending a pilot program.

Resource conservation and development were topics Freeman returned to regularly. The February 26 column recounted establishment of the Minnesota Water Resources Board, an early effort to coordinate information, hold hearings, analyze conditions, and prepare status reports on water resources. Freeman described political jockeying among agencies over turf issues and listed the major departments and agencies with claims on turf, that is, authority over water resources. They included the Water Pollution Control Commission, the State Board of Health, the Department of Conservation (now the Department of Natural Resources), and the competing interests of the Division of Waters and of Fish and Wildlife, the Soil Conservation Commission, the Water Resources Board, and the Iron Range Resources and Rehabilitation Agency.

Freeman reviewed seven major proposals submitted for legislative action in 1957 in the March 12 column. These included brief discussions of a more equitable tax structure, education, welfare (especially the needs of the elderly), conservation (especially water), standards for workers (especially safety), highway safety, and government organization and efficiency.

The March 19 column examined the work of the Governor's Committee on Exceptional Children, explaining that 50,000 of the state's children were both gifted and handicapped. "Only one out of four get the educational opportunities adequate for their needs," Freeman said. As a result, a new Division of Special Education was being established within the Department of Education to provide specialized guidance services.

Paying for government services was the topic for the March 26 weekly column, an extraordinarily detailed discussion of property-tax reforms included in recommendations from the Governor's Tax Study Committee. It had examined the inequities of the personal property tax and suggested the reduction or elimination of the most inequitable features in 13 classes at a cost of $24 million. These included business inventories, farm equipment and livestock, and household goods. Freeman's discussion of tax policy continued in the April 2 column, touching on the repeal of a five-dollar-per-head tax, describing proposed changes in the exempt status for nonresidents, and explaining the proposed elimination of penalties on married couples that had crept in inadvertently. Freeman made the point that the adoption of tax reforms depended on the adoption of withholding, an outcome that was not to be.

As the 1957 legislative session wound in April towards its 90-day-limit, the conflict over payroll withholding threatened to force a special session for complete action on the biennial budget. In 1957, however, the spending package easily could be financed with existing tax revenues. Freeman, recognizing that a fight about how the state collected taxes would not stir voter passions, reluctantly withdrew the committee's recommendations, and the legislature adopted the tax bill without withholding. Believing the logjam on legislation mainly was due to the 90-day-session limit, the legislature adopted a constitutional amendment extending the legislative session to 120 days. The April 23 column discussed the proposed amendment that voters would decide in the 1958 elections in the context of the debate on withholding. As events later proved, the logjam in the Minnesota's legislature occurs because a compromise on tax policy requires the pressure of a deadline.[12]

On May 7 Freeman reported that the 1957 legislature had authorized five new state parks—historical Frontenac, Kathio on Lake Mille Lacs, Cascade River, Temperance River Gorge, and Arrowhead River Bois Brule. Freeman said the new facilities would help ease camping pressure on state parks, which with the organized camping for groups and picnicking had increased 400 percent in ten years.

In the May 14 column he noted that the legislature had enacted more than 1,000 new statutes and mused that few people would ever know the content of all of them. Some new laws served the interest of a few individuals or industries, but some, such as that authorizing controlled access to state highways, were important to all Minnesotans. The legislature also rejected needed legislation, including proposals for mandatory seat belts.

The weekly column for May 21 turned to an issue close to Freeman. "My own deeply personal experience in rehabilitation, both as a wounded marine and in establishing rehabilitation programs for wounded and handicapped marines, convinced me that expanded activities in rehabilitation will repay Minnesota many times over." He explained that the Minnesota Department of Education operated rehabilitation programs in 12 district offices funded with federal and state funds. The cost was an investment rather than an expenditure, he said, predicting that the number of cases, doubling from 1955 to 1957, would continue to increase rapidly.

On May 28 the governor's column, returning to the March 29 topic of exceptional children, reported on legislation authorizing special-education programs. The law required school districts to provide special classes, home instruction, and hospital instruction for mentally and physically handicapped children. State reimbursements to local districts, Freeman said, would cover special-education teachers and increase reimbursements for each child. The legislature also authorized increased funding for state colleges and the University of Minnesota for teacher training and for research.

Vocational rehabilitation was again the subject for the June 3 column. Freeman explained that the state would recover the cost of vocational rehabilitation within three years in the income taxes paid by persons receiving the training. The benefits to state and federal government would not begin to compare with larger gains. A sense of worth and self-reliance cannot be measured. Society would gain by demonstrating that it could not afford to waste individual potential. Employers would benefit from a reliable workforce with fewer absentees and workplace injuries.

The July 9 column reviewed the status of old-age-assistance programs, questioning the value and purpose of ceilings, or maximums:

Since grants do not exceed bare minimum needs to maintain decent standards of living, the setting of a maximum violates our principles that no person should have to exist on a standard that is less than minimum need. If we must have a maximum, then it should be high enough to meet those needs.

On July 23 he continued to examine old-age assistance (OAA), noting that with rising medical-care costs, the payment for nursing care accounted for 40 percent of OAA costs in Minnesota. The state would pay according to need, with no limit. "Providing less than need would be unthinkable," Freeman said. Preventive care was the long-term answer, but in the short term the best answer was the provision of adequate nursing-home facilities. He lamented the legislature's rejection of a proposal for state assistance to local communities to build nursing-home facilities. Private nursing-home operators had blocked the action, illustrating the conflict between care and profit.

The July 30 column is a classic demonstration of advocacy: Freeman briefly explained the needs, cited illustrative data, and described a public program, all in the context of public duty. He examined services to mentally retarded children, describing the Minnesota program that was created by the legislature in 1915–16 and noting that crippled children were included in 1921–22. He observed that 35 years then passed before 1957 improvements brought in disturbed children and those with special behavioral problems. The program mandate now required school districts to provide special classes to children who could benefit—socially, emotionally, and physically. He applauded a 10 percent increase in per-student assistance but asked whether the increase was enough: "Special education is an obligation for any humane society to help children who face life with handicaps through no fault of their own."

Employment of the handicapped was the topic of August 12. The program meant to encourage the hire of handicapped persons was not working. Freeman told of appointing a committee with representatives from business, labor, insurance, and medicine. The problem was fear of higher insurance costs, an attitude growing from a belief that the handicapped person was prone to injury. As a result, the legislature adopted in 1957 a measure limiting employer-insurance liability to 104 weeks of disability coverage. A second state injury fund picked up liability costs after that. The changes eased the reluctance of employers to hire handicapped workers and allowed the state to achieve its goal of maximum development of human resources.

The September 2 column expressed Freeman's delight in finding administrative ways to improve government efficiency, a lifelong passion. He described the introduction of automation and electronic technology, especially Remington Rand and IBM computers, to process state tax returns. By 1957 one supervisor and four punch-card operators could use the new machines to check all the returns for accuracy in the same time that 17 examiners had taken in the past to spot-check only 75 percent of the returns.

Conservation, or the environment, was the topic for the columns of September 17 and October 1. The first described the work of the Bureau of Fisheries in the Department of Conservation, including research and management programs in fish rearing, the life history of species, natural reproduction, and feeding habits. The October 1 column examined the Bureau of Game Management, where reorganization had resulted in greater responsibility for field-level operations. A regional director was responsible for managing wildlife habitat and programs to save wetlands in each of four regions in Minnesota.

Freeman turned to a more personal concern on October 8. "If you find the governor is not available for community events on weekends this winter, the reason is the Freeman Winter Schedule," he wrote. From now until spring, "Sunday is going to be family day for the Freemans, time for Mrs. Freeman and me to spend time with our children." In fact, for the rest of his term as governor, Freeman rarely attended Sunday events. When he did, the activities almost always included picnics or other family-oriented programs.

On November 12, the eve of the start of the 1957 deer season, the governor examined the 1956 hunting season. Minnesota hunters had bagged 3.5 million game birds and animals that year. These included 70,000 deer, a million each of pheasants and waterfowl, and 370,000 grouse. Game is a dividend crop from farmlands dedicated to timber and agriculture, Freeman said, one thriving on land areas used by timber owners and farmers. Space was the problem in 1957, because of intensive farming and timber harvesting utilizing land for primary uses. Game biologists were focusing on methods to include wild game in land-use patterns and on research to develop improved practices.

Instead of hunting game, Freeman began to hunt in Japan for ways to develop trade opportunities for Minnesota companies and industries. He was the first Minnesota governor to lead a trade mission to Japan, and his November 19 column described the work of that delegation. In typical style, the column first presented a detailed account of Japan. For instance, "Japan produces 80 percent of its food needs for 90 million people on 15 percent of its land mass. Japan needs to import food, much of what Minnesota produces, including soybeans, milk, and dairy products."

Without recounting his first experiences on meeting the Japanese, Freeman's November 26 column provided a more personal account of the mission. He noted that "the miracle of Japan is the massive food aid to Japan at the start of the American occupation." He described his surprise at the treatment of Japanese women as "inferior to me." He said the Japanese press was deeply interested during press conferences when Jane Freeman, his wife, explained the work of American women, dispelling the impression that they were coddled and spoiled.

The columns were just one of the several instruments Freeman employed in casting the DFL as a party substantially different after 1954 than before. Before his arrival, the DFL was a political vehicle through which individuals campaigned together as alternatives to other, mostly Republican candidates. Through Freeman, the DFL emerged as a cohesive political party with a compelling message of pragmatic liberalism and a commanding sense of ethical governance. The DFL in the 1950s was a party challenging conventional wisdom and offering a different vision of how the world could be organized.[13]

Freeman infused governance with a sense of compassion and identified the DFL as a party of compassion. The political philosophy of the party in the 1950s was consistent with Freeman's view that all human conditions can be improved through the practice of democratic governance in which each person has an equal voice. With Freeman, the voters got a leader who believed that politics could make a difference, that politics could be a fun and robust experience, an opportunity to create public services infused with compassion. He proposed a tax policy based on the ideal that citizens contribute what they are able and receive according to their needs. He said government officials should do for others as if they were in the place of those they served. In Albert Lea, he acted to preserve the community as a place where children could grow up in peace. He said every child must have the opportunity for an excellent education. In his proposal for withholding he wished the tax burden to be fairly spread. He said the belief that income must be no barrier to good health is good health policy.

In 1960 Freeman lost his campaign for governor to the GOP's Elmer L. Andersen by fewer than 20,000 of 1.4 million votes cast. He was the sole defeated DFL incumbent on the state ballot, which troubled him almost as much as losing. John F. Kennedy carried Minnesota that year, gaining the margin of electoral college votes by which he won the presidency. Elections that close are godsends to the political experts who can discuss endlessly what tipped the scale because no one will ever know for sure. Perhaps by 1960 Minnesota voters had come to believe that Freeman possessed managerial skills and competency greater than needed. Or some may have viewed his decisiveness as impatience and become frightened by it. Freeman's actions in Albert Lea had brought a desirable outcome, particularly for the work-

175

ers with seniority, who deserved the protection of collective bargaining. But limiting the corporate freedom to destroy unions raised concern among some voters.

President Kennedy had achieved election with a narrow margin among Minnesota voters, not all of whom relished the lecture by a Lutheran governor that Protestants should put aside their religious prejudices when voting for president. In like manner the struggle over withholding, a policy strongly supported by voters, had dismayed those who found the carnage of political combat unseemly. On these and other issues, Freeman would not or could not disguise his competence in governance. Neither could he disguise his joy in politics as a contact sport, which may help explain his narrow loss in 1960.

Introducing the belief and practice of compassion as a political leitmotif in governance also carried uncertain risks. Compassion is the obverse of the status quo, of practices of discrimination still acceptable in the 1950s. A party of compassion is open to all, but it requires the participant to cast off a world of conventional comparisons—"I may not be wealthy, but I am not black." Or "I am not an Indian, I am not a woman, I am not poor, and I am not like others who are inferior to me." Freeman's rejection of discrimination, like his rejection of unethical behavior, was visceral. He made compassion an ethos of Minnesota politics.[14]

Freeman charted a course for Minnesota governance that became a roadmap for public programs and policies over the next three decades. The unhappy fate of the one-term governors who followed in the 1960s perhaps suggests he was dismissed too soon.[15] But elections are always about the future. If Minnesota voters deliver sometimes-ambiguous mandates, they rarely view elections as a means to express appreciation to those who have governed well. There is little question Freeman was ready for larger challenges. He had governed well, the time had come to move on, and so he did.

As governor and head of the DFL, Freeman achieved the goal of building a political party that Minnesota voters accepted as capable of governing with compassion. He accomplished five essential objectives:

1. The emergence of a political party that could achieve critical political mass, a consensus among economic, social, cultural, and community interests, with a majority of at least one vote.
2. The DFL's creation of policy momentum in critical sectors:
   • governance, or program management
   • services, or social goals and programs
   • intellectual, or policy innovations
   • economic, or jobs and wealth spread widely
   • organization, or power to transform promise into reality.
3. The DFL's capacity to inform and influence key institutional audiences:
   • academics
   • the voting public
   • government institutions
   • nongovernment institutions
   • the press
   • party activists.
4. DFL status necessary to function as a coordinating mechanism for consensus.
5. The isolation of political opponents within a nonpartisan context, achieved with political objective and purpose.

Orville and Jane Freeman at home in Minneapolis in 1999

—8—

Epilogue[1]

The Minnesota Senate in 1957 rejected the tax-reform recommendations of the Governor's Tax Study Committee appointed by Gov. Orville L. Freeman. This effectively destroyed the prospects for a rational debate on tax policy. Lacking a consensus or even a coherent philosophy, Minnesota legislators in the 1960s allowed tax policy to drift even as it dominated the political agenda of the state. Conflict was inevitable.

Minnesota tax policy is clear on only one point: The state constitution mandates that the governor present a balanced budget to the legislature. In turn, the lawmakers must enact a balanced budget. This means the identification of revenue sources to cover spending programs—and no deficits. Political campaigns of the time did not reflect the conflict over tax policy but instead left the impression of consensus. Neither the GOP nor the DFL proposed adoption of a sales tax in party platforms of the 1950s and 1960s. Between 1954 and 1970, every sitting governor—of DFL or GOP persuasion—campaigned on the promise to veto a sales tax. Special sessions to resolve arguments over who picked up the check for public services—some brief and others of historic duration—followed all but two legislative sessions in that period. The argument was always about where the tax burden would fall.

Minnesota was growing, and the state's economy was moving in new directions. The educational demands for an emerging economy based on science and technology imposed new disciplines on state universities that raised funding pressures on state government. Funding needs for schools, welfare, and public services were fast increasing. Funding requests regularly outpaced the revenues available to new legislative sessions. Where would new funds be found? To examine that question, the Governor's Tax Study Committee offered a process for evaluating the effects of tax choices on several factors, including fairness, balance, ability to pay, the impact on the competitiveness of Minnesota industries and companies, and other long-term conditions. The committee did not recommend specific tax options other than that the state reduce its reliance on property taxes.

For some, the question was not open to debate. Minnesota in the 1950s did not use a sales tax, and some believed the only issue was when the legislature would adopt such a tax. The Minnesota press, especially the metropolitan newspapers, blew this policy ember to a constant blaze. The *Minneapolis Star* and *Tribune* and the *St. Paul Dispatch* and *Pioneer Press* shared a common position with the sales-tax wing of the Minnesota Republican Party, heavily rural in character, that controlled the Conservative caucuses of the legislature.

The sales-tax wing of the GOP, representing Minnesota corporate and business interests including the Minnesota Farm Bureau, was regularly thwarted by its inability to control the selection of GOP candidates for governor. Neither Elmer L. Andersen, elected in 1960, nor Harold LeVander, elected in 1966, was an organizational Republican. Both considered opposition to a sales tax an essential strategy in winning elections. Their position ensured that a pro-sales-tax GOP candidate would lack the political support to win endorsement at the GOP state convention or in a primary fight. The ambivalence within the GOP over a sales tax also led to a heavily conditioned position on tax policy in Republican Party platforms.

The DFL opposed a sales tax, preferring to rely on a tax on income as the primary revenue source for Minnesota government. The DFL position was the central feature of opposition to the sales tax within the executive branch of Minnesota government, which provided the political muscle to sustain a veto. The DFL, reflecting the policies espoused by Freeman for a progressive tax system built around a tax on income, consistently and publicly opposed the sales tax as a regressive burden on low- and moderate-income families. The DFL saw no conflict or political struggle around tax policy.

Enactment of a sales tax was possible under only two circumstances: the election of a veto-proof Conservative majority in favor of the sales-tax program or the persuasion of a Republican governor to recant on a campaign pledge. In 1961 control of the legislature was divided, with a DFL House majority and a Conservative, or Republican, majority in the Senate. The Senate, mindful that it faced reelection in 1963, was in no mood to replay the bruising confrontation over tax policy that had led to the longest special session in Minnesota history in 1959.[2] In 1961 the Senate would not follow Sen. Donald O. Wright, Minneapolis, over a political precipice as it had when two years earlier, as chair of the Senate tax committee, he failed to impose a sales tax in a test of wills with Governor Freeman. Instead, the Senate agreed with the House early in the 1961 session to adopt withholding and legislate the forgiveness of a full year's tax liability—that is, 100 percent of taxes owed on wages and earnings in 1962 or 1963, whichever was less.[3]

As the end of the 1961 session came into sight, however, the legislature had not resolved a revenue gap of $61 million. Wrangling between the House and the Senate over education funding levels and revenue sources had stalled efforts to close the session in the 90 days allotted by the state constitution. Behind the scenes, sales-tax advocates were busy at work. As chair of the Senate tax committee, Wright had introduced a 3 percent sales-tax proposal in the waning days of the session. But after DFL senators called for a recorded vote on procedures to take up the measure, the committee withdrew its report from action on the Senate floor. Conservatives did not want to go on record in support of a sales tax. As in 1959, with revenue issues still hanging, the legislature faced a special session called by Governor Andersen for Monday, April 24.[4] While Andersen was preparing for his address to a joint session of the House and Senate on Tuesday, the Minnesota Farm Bureau began lobbying for a 3 percent sales-tax proposal. Andersen renewed his opposition to a sales tax, a position the *Minneapolis Tribune* editorially lamented as an impediment resulting from "campaign promises he felt obligated to continue."[5]

Fred A. Cina, House DFL (majority) leader, said the sales tax was dead for the 1961 legislature. A week later Senate Majority Leader Stanley Holmquist agreed.[6] The legislature could close out the revenue deficit of an estimated $61 million by adopting 50 percent forgiveness for withholding.[7] The *Minneapolis Tribune,* ever hopeful, editorialized that the legislature should "take the sales tax now."[8]

Thus the Senate tax committee adopted a tax bill without a sales-tax provision; it relied on taking back 50 percent of the withholding windfall plus a 1 percent tax on adjusted gross income. Harold Schultz, Senate minority leader, described the measure "as a head tax in a lousy tax package," a view echoed by D. D. Wozniak, chair of the House tax committee. The proposal was "the most irresponsible and sorry tax bill ever returned from the Senate," Wozniak said in launching the political ritual that accompanies legislative negotiations on tax measures. The House reenacted its original tax package to raise $61 million in new revenues while retaining 100 percent forgiveness. The legislative stalemate continued through May, largely due to disagreements over education spending.

Five weeks after the special session began, the legislature agreed to a spending package on education. At the same time it rejected a parallel initiative supported by Governor Andersen and Speaker of the House Cina to cap taxes on taconite in exchange for investments of $200 million by the steel industry within the next six years. With these controversies resolved, the House and Senate conference committee could meet to settle differences in the tax packages of the two bodies. After pleading for withholding for six years, the House DFL conferees did not miss the irony of the Conservative position; they proposed dropping the head tax in exchange for a 75 percent forgiveness provision in withholding. The Senate accepted.[9]

If, assuming Andersen's reelection, the sales-tax lobby hoped for a change in his views on a sales tax in the 1963 legislative session, the longest recount and closest race for governor in Minnesota history put an end to it.[10] Lt. Gov. Karl Rolvaag, 1962 DFL-endorsed candidate for governor in 1962, unseated Andersen in a campaign that ended in a virtual tie. Rolvaag was certified as the winner by a margin of 95 votes after a four-month recount of 1.4 million ballots.

Minnesota tax receipts in 1963 benefited from a strong national economy, and tax-policy issues receded, making for a relatively benign legislative session. Tempers changed in 1965, however, as Governor Rolvaag proposed a $609 million budget in which overall education spending would grow to $343 million for the 1966–67 biennium. Included in a welfare-program spending proposal of $172.6 million was a request for 272 new staff positions for mental-health care in state hospitals. Rolvaag asked for a $52 million increase in income taxes to close revenue deficits for the biennium. In 1965 Conservatives controlled both the House and Senate, but not by the two-thirds margin required to override a governor's veto. The legislature, however, dallied in resolving the revenue deficit, forcing Rolvaag to call a special session, during which he deflated a Conservative effort to float a sales-tax proposal by threatening a veto. The House adopted a tax plan to raise $52 million in new funds by increasing income-tax levels. The Senate accepted the House proposal with one change—limiting the increase in income taxes to the 1966–67 biennium, a feature introduced by Senator Wright, chair of the Senate tax committee. The House agreed, and the 1965 legislature adjourned sine die.

Rolvaag's term as governor was stormy, more for the internal dissension arising in the DFL than for any conflict with the legislature. An influx of new leaders, talented individuals with political ambitions attracted by the DFL breakthrough to prominence in the 1950s, chafed under Rolvaag's sometimes inconsistent and unpredictable behavior.[11] Led by Lt. Gov. Sandy Keith, elected in 1962 on the DFL ticket with Rolvaag, the DFL convention in June 1966 rejected Rolvaag for endorsement for reelection, an unprecedented action. The convention chose Keith as the DFL candidate instead. Refusing to accept the decision of the state convention, Rolvaag ran against Keith in the September primary, winning the DFL endorsement handily. The DFL, in a shambles, lost the top state offices and control of the House and the Senate that November, setting the stage for a Minnesota sales tax. The GOP candidate, Harold LeVander, won with a 52 percent majority—680,000 votes to Rolvaag's 608,000. The Republican tide was strong enough to elect a Republican governor and provide Conservative caucuses of more than a two-thirds majority in both the House and the Senate.

The business community and most Minnesota newspapers viewed the election of a Conservative majority large enough to override any veto as an opportunity to enact a state sales tax. And as subsequent events proved, the sales-tax wing of the Republican Party did not view Harold LeVander as the leader of the Republican Party. He had promised, if elected, to veto sales-tax legislation unless it included provisions for a voter referendum in the election following passage of the legislation.[12] Both LeVander and the sales-tax lobby knew that voters would never approve a new tax, especially one shifting the tax burden to small taxpayers. LeVander could tell his friends who supported a sales tax that he did not oppose their proposal. He could also tell his friends who opposed a sales tax that he knew the legislature would never pass a bill with little prospect of approval in a referendum.

Rarely in politics and never on issues of passion and partisanship does a candidate get the best of both worlds. The sales-tax issue proved the rule that the fence is the worst possible place in Minnesota for a new governor to sit. LeVander came into office with prospects for becoming a highly popular leader. He had inherited a surplus of $115 million from the outgoing DFL administration, primarily from the two-year increase in income-tax rates enacted under Rolvaag in 1965. LeVander proposed a $104 million tax-relief package to lower property taxes for individuals and businesses. He asked the legislature to raise to nearly 50 percent the state's share of local school costs. He proposed a record state-building program. All of this, LeVander said, could be done without new taxes or an increase in tax rates.[13]

Governor LeVander was laying out an agenda likely to assure Republican control of state government for the next eight years or longer, not an impossible task. Traditionally the governor is considered the leader of his political party. As further proof of his wisdom, LeVander could point to the disarray in the DFL, a political enterprise prone to shooting itself in the foot.

Apparently no one was listening, especially not the sales-tax wing of his party. Soon after LeVander's inauguration, the sales-tax tide swept him away. Conservatives in the House, dominated by a veto-proof Conservative majority, introduced a plethora of sales-tax bills.[14] A 4 percent sales-tax proposal followed a bill for a 3 percent sales tax, both competing with a general excise-tax bill of 2.5 percent and a 3.5 percent gross-receipts tax proposal. Recommendations for the repeal of property taxes accompanied them.

Meanwhile in the Senate chambers, Sen. Donald O. Wright, chair of the tax committee and a longtime sales-tax advocate, patiently waited for the House, where tax and spending proposals originate, to act. The Minnesota Poll reported on Sunday, April 28, that 57 percent of voting age Minnesotans opposed the sales tax.[15] On Tuesday, two days later, the floodgates opened on the sales-tax drive. In a front-page story spread like a declaration of war across the top half of the newspaper, the *Minneapolis Tribune* revealed that the Citizens League of Minneapolis had endorsed a 3 percent sales tax.[16] The proposal had been prepared in detail by a committee co-chaired by David Graven, a University of Minnesota law professor and DFL finance chair, and John Mardy, a Minneapolis attorney and a Republican.[17]

The Citizens League sales-tax proposal earmarked two-thirds of the revenues for school districts and local government in lieu of property taxes. An $18-per-person credit on state income taxes would ease the regressive nature of a sales tax. The proposal mandated a six-dollar income-tax credit per person for each additional 1 percent hike in the sales tax. Governor LeVander liked the league's sales-tax proposal.[18]

A week after featuring the Citizens League proposal, the *Minneapolis Tribune* published a new Minnesota Poll reporting that a majority of Minnesotans favored the Graven-Mardy sales-tax plan but continued to oppose a general sales tax. Senator Wright said he was studying the Citizens League proposal.[19]

The sales tax was riding on a floodtide of Republican support by mid-May. On May 16 the House adopted a 3 percent sales tax on a party-line vote.[20] Governor LeVander said he would veto the House bill. The Senate tax committee rejected the House bill a day later but adopted Senator Wright's proposal for a 3 percent excise tax.[21] DFL minorities in both the House and Senate strongly opposed the Conservatives' tax proposals. A House and Senate conference committee met quickly and agreed to recommend a 3 percent excise tax, which the House adopted on May 19.[22] The Senate swiftly followed suit, sending the tax bill to Governor LeVander for an expected veto.

LeVander vetoed the bill quickly, leaving the House and Senate one day to override his veto.[23] On May 20 the Senate DFL minority, led by Sen. Karl Grittner of St. Paul, blocked Senate action to override the veto through procedural tactics until the regular session of the legislature expired at midnight.[24]

The following day Governor LeVander announced a special session of the legislature to begin May 23. Upon the opening of the special session, the Conservative Senate majority immediately adopted new procedural rules to strip the minority DFL caucus of its ability to delay sales-tax votes. Then the Senate joined with the House to listen to Governor LeVander's message.[25]

LeVander proposed a tax bill containing many of the features of a DFL tax package, including a $102.5 million property-tax relief package that would take $73 million from the state's tax surplus, a 5 percent luxury tax, and a 7 percent increase in corporate income taxes. He said the proposal "provides substantial relief and reform without major new taxes or imposing large tax increases." The governor promised to veto a general sales tax.[26]

The House voted two days later to adopt a 3 percent excise tax with Conservatives providing all but a handful of the 90 votes cast for the measure, exactly the number needed for an override of the expected veto.[27] A day later the Senate followed suit with a similar bill and recessed for the weekend.[28] The following Monday a conference committee agreed to resolve minor differences between the two tax measures, recommending a 3 percent excise tax.[29] Since the opening day of the special session, Governor LeVander had been pleading with Conservative legislators to break away from the excise-tax proposal of the Republican majority and to support his veto. While the DFL minority caucuses had said they would support his veto, LeVander was unable to get any support from his fellow Republicans.

Governor LeVander vetoed the 3 percent excise tax June 1, and the Conservative majority of the legislature immediately voted to override, enacting the first major change in Minnesota tax law since the 1933 adoption of a state income tax.[30]

The excise/sales tax significantly lowered personal property and property taxes for homeowners, farmers, and corporations, partly through lower business-inventory taxes. The legislature allocated $64 million each to the income-tax fund supporting education programs and to the general-revenue fund. The legislation excluded food, clothing, drugs, gasoline, and services from the sales tax. But the provision for individual credits to allow income-tax deductions, first proposed by the Minneapolis Citizens League, did not survive. Conservatives claimed that taxpayers would annually receive 35 percent relief on property taxes from sales-tax receipts.

The Republican tax-chickens came home to roost in 1969. Senator Wright complained that Minnesota counties had increased property-tax rates 50 percent more than the legislature and the state tax department had expected, emptying the sales-tax fund for property-tax relief.[31] Stanley Holmquist, Senate majority leader, added to the confusion by declaring that the sales-tax fund for property-tax relief faced a $100 million deficit within two years.[32] LeVander said the cost of higher-than-anticipated local tax rises forced him to raise expenditures for the biennium by $17 million. He also said he would shift the date of payment to local governments for property-tax relief into the succeeding fiscal year to prevent a $98 million deficit.[33] Holmquist explained the one-time sleight-of-hand maneuver by noting that the deficit apparently was put off in perpetuity. He said the procedural delay was preferable to paying funds from sales-tax revenues on time, which would require immediate new taxes.

The Great Tax War consuming Minnesota for 15 years sputtered to an unsatisfactory end as the 1960s came to a close. No gubernatorial candidate and no sitting governor had campaigned for a sales tax. Neither political party had campaigned for a sales tax. Minnesota had a sales tax but no coherent tax policy. How did it happen? Minnesota voters would have to sort out these events and decide who could best serve their political future. The answer was clear.

In 1970, the voters chose Wendell Anderson, the DFL candidate for governor, along with Conservative majorities in both the House and the Senate. The Senate was almost evenly split, with 34 Conservatives and 33 DFL members. Two years later, following redistricting to reflect the 1970 census, control of the House had swung to the DFL caucus of 77 members as opposed to 57 Conservatives. The DFL also became the majority caucus in the Senate, increasing its membership to 37 while the number of Conservatives dropped to 30.

Governor Anderson's inaugural message was conventional, overshadowed by a political donnybrook in the Senate. Anderson said his administration would focus on four areas—drug control, housing, legislative reform, and environmental protection. The latter, he said, would be his first concern.[34] He also proposed a constitutional amendment to authorize annual sessions of the legislature.

President of the Senate and DFL Lt. Gov. Rudy Perpich had exploded a political bomb. He ruled that the DFL would organize the Senate even though the Conservative caucus had 34 members compared to the DFL's 33. The election of Sen. Richard F. Palmer, Duluth, was in dispute, Perpich ruled. He refused to swear in Palmer. With both caucuses tied at 33, Perpich then ruled to recognize the DFL caucus as the majority. This decision also gave the DFL the authority to decide disputed elections. Conservatives immediately challenged Perpich's rulings in the Minnesota Supreme Court, which, some three weeks later, resolved the issue by recognizing the election of Palmer.[35]

Nothing had prepared the legislature or the public, however, for the stunning surprise Anderson unveiled in his budget message at the end of January.[36] He asked for a tax increase of $728 million for the 1972–73 biennium. More than half the increase, some $390 million, was to replace property taxes in a dramatic overhaul of public-school financing. Overall spending in the biennium would jump nearly a third, from $2.3 billion in the 1970–71 biennium to nearly $3 billion. While earlier legislatures had pledged state revenues to provide at least 50 percent of public-school operating expenses, Anderson said, property taxes were generating 57 percent of local school revenues. The State of Minnesota would shoulder 64 percent of those costs in 1972 under his proposal, he explained, and 70 percent in 1973.

With that announcement, the *Minneapolis Star* noted, the governor had introduced tax policy as the centerpiece of his budget and legislative program for 1971. The bold financial initiative also contained other surprises. Anderson proposed $100-per-pupil support for students in private and parochial schools at a cost of $27 million. He proposed increased revenue sharing with municipalities and higher salary schedules for state employees. He also asked for significant increases in state scholarships and grants in aid, a new scholarship program for American Indians, and higher spending for vocational rehabilitation. Anderson also proposed reducing personal-property taxes on business.

The boldness of Governor Anderson's initiative was all the more astonishing with the perspective of time. According to a *New York Times* survey of 50 states and representative cities in 1971, a majority of the states and municipalities of the time had severe revenue problems leading to cuts in spending and/or sharp tax increases.[37] Many states also were looking to federal revenue-sharing, though with little enthusiasm for proposals by President Richard Nixon from states that would do better under current federal grants in aid.

As required by the state constitution, Governor Anderson said he would raise $600 million in additional revenues from personal and corporate income taxes. The remainder would come from a variety of excise taxes, primarily a nine-cent-per-pack increase on cigarettes. Anderson did not mention the sales tax. He warned he would not approve a tax bill "unless it provides substantial property-tax relief."

Conservative legislators were flatfooted, caught between Governor Anderson's commitment to the reform of education funding and the promise of substantial property-tax relief in a state where two of every three families owned their homes. Richfield's Ernest Lindstrom, Conservative House majority leader, called the budget proposal "reckless," complaining that Anderson awarded pay increases to public employees without regard to merit and did not propose cuts in welfare.[38]

The budget proposal, a daring political maneuver, grasped a policy initiative that remained firmly in Anderson's control for the legislative session. The Conservatives struggled to respond but succeeded only in plunging the legislature into the longest special session in Minnesota history. Controlling both houses, the Conservatives nevertheless became locked in an internal struggle pitting the Minnesota Senate in a public battle over tax policy against the Minnesota House. The governor, along with the rest of Minnesota, simply watched from the sidelines. Upon the legislature's deadlock at the end of the regular session, Anderson called a special session in May. May gave way to June, which passed into July and the eighth week without resolution of the tax question among Conservative legislators.

The Senate, split almost evenly between DFLers and Conservatives, in early July adopted a tax plan hewing closely to Anderson's proposal in the amount of new revenues.[39] The Senate proposed to raise $677 million, differing primarily in the inclusion of a 1 percent increase in the state sales tax. Anderson said raising the level of the general sales tax was acceptable because a "significant" reduction in property taxes could be achieved.

The House rejected the Senate's proposal, extending the special session further while conferees from both bodies attempted to find a tax policy on which Conservatives could agree. Senate Conservatives began to narrow their differences with House Conservatives through July, primarily by agreeing to the regressive features adopted by the House. By July 27 the conferees agreed on a bill to raise $599 million in new revenues that Governor Anderson promptly vetoed.[40] "The idea that the most powerful and wealthy should get the most tax relief is unacceptable," Anderson said. "This is a very bad bill that suits the demands of special interests." He cited the liquor and steel industries as special benefactors. Anderson called for a bipartisan legislative commission to resolve the tax issue. Since both the House and the Senate had approved the Conservative tax bill with only razor-thin margins, neither branch tried to override Anderson's veto.

The House and Senate reluctantly returned to chambers to await further deliberations of the tax conference committee as all hell broke loose. The Minnesota Board of Education warned that some districts might face insolvency as they began preparing budgets for the school year starting in September. They wanted to know how much state aid to expect. The state employees' union, representing more than one-fourth of state employees, began preparing to strike in the absence of a contract. *Apollo 15,* blasting off for the moon July 23, returned August 6 as the tax conferees met in futile session. As the deadlock continued into September, Roland Hatfield, state auditor, warned that the stand-off threatened the state's cash flow and could affect its credit rating.[41]

By early October, with the drafting help of (DFL) House Minority Leader Martin Sabo, a compromise tax bill was in the works. The proposal sought to raise $581 million in new tax revenues, with higher personal and corporate income taxes providing $341 million. A 1 percent increase in general sales-tax rates and higher excise taxes accounted for most of the rest. School districts could expect a 67 percent increase in state aid, while municipal government coffers would rise by 29 percent. Both measures were to produce significantly lower property taxes.[42]

The House and the Senate, with strong DFL support over Conservative opposition, approved the tax bill on October 28; Governor Anderson signed it on October 30.[43] The legislature adjourned sine die at 2:30 the next morning, some 157 days after the start of the special 1971 session. This was more than twice the length of the previous record—a 68-day special session in 1959. It remains today the longest special session in Minnesota history.

The *Minneapolis Tribune* said the adopted tax program was "a major legislative accomplishment," citing a "substantial increase in the state share of school costs, reform of the state school aid formula, a new formula for revenue sharing as municipal aid, and a significant reduction in property taxes." Legislators left wearily for home, the campaign of 1972 almost immediately to follow. How would Minnesota voters respond to their work? Would they punish the legislature for the long special session or reward it for a historic and innovative policy on taxes and public services? Which party might they credit, or which would they blame?

In 1972 the DFL won control of both the House and the Senate for the first time in 114 years. Two years later, the answer became even clearer; the DFL gained an astonishing 72-vote majority in the House and increased its majority in the Senate to ten. The voters re-elected Governor Anderson by a record margin. His bold shift of Minnesota's tax structure from reliance on property taxes, while substantially enlarging the financial resources devoted to education and social services, was a textbook example of tax policy as a creative force. The political consequences rewarded the use of political leadership of a dynamic process of democratic governance to translate consensus on goals into policies and programs.

Political leadership, however, is both a personal quality and an institutional capacity. Over the 17 years from 1954, when Orville L. Freeman became the first DFL governor, to 1971, when Wendell Anderson made tax-policy history, the DFL gained the public trust for governing responsibly and effectively. It established a tradition of communicating its goals clearly to Minnesotans and delivered on its commitments in a disciplined manner. The remarkable achievements in tax policy and social programs of 1971 could not have occurred without the gutsy and brilliant leadership of Gov. Wendell Anderson. Neither would they have been realized without the trust accorded the DFL, achieved by its emergence through the vision of Gov. Orville Freeman as the party best representing the consensus of Minnesota voters.

Orville L. Freeman, 84, died in Minneapolis on Thursday, February 20, 2003, due to complications from Alzheimer's disease. He was survived by Jane Shields Freeman, his wife of 61 years; his daughter, Constance, of Nairobi, Kenya; his son, Michael Orville; his daughter-in-law, Theresa; and three grandchildren, Katie, Beth, and Matthew.

Memorial observances were held in the Rotunda of the Minnesota State Capitol and at Mount Olivet Lutheran Church in Minneapolis. The burial was private. The family welcomes gifts to the Jane and Orville Freeman International Center of the Humphrey Institute at the University of Minnesota and to the Walker Health Center Foundation for Alzheimer's Program, in Minneapolis.

References

Sources mentioned in the text are not repeated here.

Abbreviations
OLF=Orville L. Freeman
MHS= Minnesota Historical Society

Chapter 1
1. Robert Cato, "The Orator of the Dawn," *The New Yorker* (March 4, 2002): 46–63.
2. Ibid.
3. Hubert H. Humphrey to OLF, November 27, 1953, OLF Papers, MHS: "Politics has a way of wearing on a guy. I get to the point where I really dislike it. [I]f I were to honestly state my conviction, I suppose it would be that I like it for its joys but detest it for its miseries, and right now the miseries seem almost more than the joy."
4. Ibid.
5. Freeman had returned to Minnesota at the close of World War II following extensive rehabilitation for a serious head wound received as a U.S. Marine lieutenant on patrol on Bougainville Island in the South Pacific. He completed law school at the University of Minnesota and became active in DFL organizational politics, assembling volunteers, veterans, women, reformers, and academic activists to wrest control of the party from former Farmer-Labor leaders in early 1946. In doing so, he resumed the friendship with Humphrey that had begun on the U of M campus before the war.

6. Freeman's mother later said that in prewar conversations with Freeman, Humphrey said he would become a senator from Minnesota. Freeman said being governor was more important. OLF interview by author, October 1998.

7. Gerald Heaney, then architect of the DFL and now judge in the U.S. Court of Appeals, believes Humphrey could have risen to the presidency only with Freeman as his chief of staff. Towards the end of his life, Humphrey acknowledged his one great mistake was failing to put Freeman unequivocally in charge of his 1968 presidential campaign. Every political leader needs at least one person to say the things he or she does not want, but needs, to hear.

8. Anderson inherited most of the third term of Gov. Luther W. Youngdahl, who unexpectedly resigned in 1951 to accept President Harry S. Truman's appointment to the federal court.

9. OLF to Hubert H. Humphrey, January 20, 1953, OLF Papers, MHS.

10. Olson died late in his third term in 1935; Farmer-Labor Lt. Gov. Elmer Benson succeeded him and ran for reelection in 1936.

11. The political shift of many U.S. voters between 1928 and 1936, the period during which New Deal Democrats became the dominant political center, reached Massachusetts a decade later, in 1948. Not until 1954 did it take place in Minnesota and other midwestern states. Massachusetts was the only state outside the four-state core of the Dixie South to vote for Al Smith, a Catholic and the Democratic candidate for president in 1928. That election, however, bonded the Democratic Party with Catholic voters. The relationship, visible only in Massachusetts, set the stage for the Roosevelt 1936 sweep in which the New Deal carried all states except Maine. See Mark C. Carnes and John A. Garraty, with Patrick Williams, *Mapping America's Past: A Historical Atlas* (New York: Henry Holt, 1966), 180–81.

12. Early in 1953 Humphrey asked his staff to organize a campaign network with a unit in each congressional district identified as a Humphrey organization. The senator enlisted party leaders including Freeman and Gerald Heaney, national Democratic committeeman from Minnesota, to assist in the operation. While Freeman and Heaney supported the idea, the network died from poor leadership. OLF, Heaney, and Humphrey correspondence, OLF Papers, MHS.

13. As the 1954 DFL convention in Albert Lea headed for showdown votes on whether to endorse candidates and on other issues of party discipline, Humphrey told reporters he would support whatever the convention decided. See *St. Paul Pioneer Press,* April 2, 1954.

14. The 1954 endorsed candidate for secretary of state was Koscie Marsh of St. Paul. Soon after the convention ended, Marsh publicly endorsed pari-mutuel betting, a position the DFL had rejected in its opposition to legalized gambling. The DFL central committee polled county and congressional district DFL chairs to gain support for a resolution revoking Marsh's endorsement,

done in a matter of days. The central committee selected Joe Donovan of Duluth to fill the vacancy. He was elected and served in the office almost 30 years. OLF Papers, MHS.

15. Behind the scenes, Humphrey acted swiftly to head off threats to the "strong ticket" reelection strategy. When in 1953 several labor officials raised a trial balloon for the gubernatorial endorsement of Paul Rasmusson, a longtime DFL operative, Humphrey wrote them a long letter explaining why the idea had no merit. Rasmusson, a member of the Railroad and Warehouse Commission, then an elective office, had been chair of the Farmer-Labor Party during its 1944 fusion with the Democrats. Humphrey warned that reopening the wounds of the merger would not help the campaigns. Hubert H. Humphrey to Duluth union officials, OLF Papers, MHS.

16. Freeman recalled that prior to the state DFL convention, Eugenie Anderson, a DFL stalwart from Red Wing, said, "Orv, you can't win, but you gotta run." She felt that would put the strongest DFL ticket in the field and help ensure Humphrey's reelection. Arthur Naftalin (former mayor of Minneapolis) interview, January 16, 1978, copy in OLF Papers, MHS.

17. News reports of the events leading to the 1954 state DFL convention referred daily to Freeman's no-campaign stance while quoting his rivals' charges of bossism. The reports never mentioned Humphrey, who used the "strong candidate" strategy. *St. Paul Pioneer Press, St. Paul Dispatch, Minneapolis Tribune,* and *Minneapolis Star,* March and April 1954.

Chapter 2

1. OLF to Hubert H. Humphrey, April 9, 1954, OLF Papers, MHS.

2. Fifteen years earlier, in the midst of the Great Depression, Freeman spent a summer hitchhiking through southern Minnesota. His family had farmed near Zumbrota, and Freeman went down country roads, from farm to farm, asking for work. He returned home to start school in the fall with more than $50, a respectable summer's wage. OLF Papers, MHS.

3. Freeman in 1953 dispatched John Bystrom, associate professor of English at the University of Minnesota and DFL office volunteer, to report on potential applications in political campaigns of the pioneering work on mass-mailing technology and fundraising methods at the Billy Graham Institute in suburban St. Paul. As a result, Freeman convinced Humphrey to give funds from his reelection campaign to the state DFL office for a machine that automatically added a candidate's signature to letters. The added authenticity was especially valuable for fundraising. Humphrey grumbled about the cost, but Freeman used the machine on all his gubernatorial correspondence.

4. Bill Kubicek interview by author, August 1999.

5. Ibid. Stanley E. Hubbard, owner of Channel 5 in the Twin Cities, refused to participate in statewide programs after the first broadcast. Kubicek quietly purchased time through other buyers for subsequent broadcasts. "You're a

sneaky one," Hubbard said to Kubicek, threatening to pull future programs in spite of existing contracts. Coming from Hubbard, Kubicek considered the epithet a compliment.

6. Bill Kubicek interview by author, August 1999.

7. Ibid. Humphrey initially was reluctant to participate in the telecast, and only a personal request from Freeman helped change his decision. Ibid.

8. Bill Kubicek interview by author, August 1999. The first statewide political telecast used three live cameras, anticipating the *I Love Lucy* television series, credited with originating the three-camera format for commercial programs.

9. Bill Kubicek interview by author, August 1999.

10. Including candidates for legislative seats on the DFL sample ballot also broke political tradition. The Minnesota Legislature was officially nonpartisan, with members joining caucuses labeled Conservative or Liberal. The sample ballot implied the DFL was prepared to be held accountable for policies affecting Minnesota voters.

11. Freeman was elected secretary of the DFL in 1946, thus gaining control of the key organizational position in its executive committee. Freeman and Eugenie Anderson of Red Wing, who was elected vice chair, were the sole survivors of a postwar reform group that had suffered a humiliating defeat by a Farmer-Labor faction over party leadership. As secretary, Freeman organized a series of political maneuvers blocking a Farmer-Labor effort led by former Gov. Elmer Benson to bolt the national Democratic Party in 1948. Benson and the Farmer-Labor faction believed they could lead the DFL into the Progressive Party and so endorse Henry Wallace for president. Ousting the Benson Farmer-Laborites in 1948, Freeman and Humphrey led the Minnesota delegation to the 1948 Democratic convention in Philadelphia that nominated Harry Truman for reelection and adopted a civil-rights plank proposed by Humphrey.

12. The decision to endorse candidates was a touchy subject for the DFL, still uneasy about the amalgamation of the Farmer-Laborites and Democrats and concerned that party discipline might appear to dictate political choice. The February 1953 DFL conference for planning the state convention had argued long over a resolution for endorsing candidates. A minority report proposed that the convention *not* endorse candidates. The party resolved the issue by granting each county, district, and state convention the choice of whether or not to endorse anyone, then amended the rules of the state convention to authorize it. DFL Central Committee Files, MHS.

13. Over the next six years, as the DFL became the dominant political force in Minnesota, Jacobson, who viewed politics as a forum for public service and was a fierce proponent of ethics in government, became the philosophical center of the party.

14. Gerald Heaney pushed Donovan to the fore. Unknown outside Duluth and Lake County, Donovan gave the DFL state ticket a Catholic candidate from

the Iron Range and visibility to Catholic voters, who constituted the largest block of traditional Democratic supporters. Donovan won the November 1954 election and served as secretary of state until retiring in 1978. Gerald Heaney interview by author, June 1999.

15. The issue of party discipline was important to political observers. By 1958, when Freeman carried the DFL to a statewide victory, the editorial page of the *Minneapolis Morning Tribune,* for November 5, 1958, lamented that "the DFL Party is better disciplined and better able to keep its members voting a straight ticket."

16. Freeman, frustrated over his loss in the gubernatorial campaign of 1952 and with no money for party organization, contemplated closing the DFL state office. In a January 14, 1953, letter to Humphrey, he suggested the space might continue as a Humphrey office. "However, this is your show, and I think it should be on that basis I carry the office for a couple of months and (with the help of others) carry it for the balance of this year if you felt this would be desirable. I have no plans, as you know, and can't afford to continue the office and will be happy to close it up." OLF Papers, MHS.

17. OLF Papers, MHS.

18. If the relationship between Freeman and Humphrey is integral to the emergence of the DFL, no less critical to its development is that between Heaney and Freeman. Heaney was legal counsel to the Duluth Central Union Council. Both were World War II combat veterans. Each possessed highly organized minds, an appetite for politics, a fearsome intolerance of incompetence, an awesome work ethic, and a commitment to public service. Their relationship endured because Heaney, notorious for detailed, precise memos with exact instructions, lived in Duluth. Had he lived in the Twin Cities, making daily contact inevitable, the relationship might not have survived.

19. OLF Papers, MHS.

20. Report, June 16, 1953, OLF Papers, MHS.

21. OLF to Humphrey, July 6, 1953. OLF Papers, MHS.

22. OLF memorandum "Comments on Meeting of Kitchen Cabinet," August 18, 1953, OLF Papers, MHS.

23. OLF to Humphrey, April 9, 1954. OLF Papers, MHS.

24. Ibid.

25. John Bystrom, designated six months earlier in a Kitchen Cabinet meeting as Humphrey's campaign manager, sent the senator a detailed memorandum on the status of the campaign, copying Mitch Perrazo, Humphrey's Minnesota staff director, Heaney, and Freeman. OLF Papers, MHS.

26. Humphrey to OLF, April 19, 1954, OLF Papers, MHS.

27. Half-page ad, *St. Paul Dispatch,* November 30, 1954, p. 9.

28. *Minneapolis Star,* October 22, 1954, p. 8.

29. *Minneapolis Tribune,* October 26, 1954, p. 1.

30. *St. Paul Dispatch,* October 27, 1954, p. 1.

31. *Minneapolis Tribune,* October 30, 1954, p. 1.
32. Ibid., October 21, 1954, p. 28.
33. *St. Paul Dispatch,* October 14, 1954, p. 1.
34. Ibid., October 18, 1954, p. 4.
35. Ibid., p. 1.
36. Ibid.
37. *Minneapolis Tribune,* October 26, 1954, p. 8.
38. *St. Paul Dispatch,* October 14, 1954, p. 25.
39. Ibid., October 20, 1954, p. 42.
40. *Minneapolis Tribune,* October 27, 1954, p. 18.
41. Ibid., editorial page.
42. *Minneapolis Tribune,* October 31, 1954, editorial page.
43. Ibid., p. 1.
44. OLF interview by author, August 1999.
45. The explanation of how Freeman received the scars on his face quietly laid to rest a rumor that the scars were the result of a barroom fight.
46. *Minneapolis Star,* November 12, 1954, p. 12.
47. *Minneapolis Tribune,* November 28, 1954, p. 2.

Chapter 3

1. *Minneapolis Tribune,* November 14, 1955, p. 1.
2. Arvonne Fraser interview by author, May 1999.
3. *Minneapolis Tribune,* November 15, 1954, p. 15.
4. Ibid., November 17, 1954. p. 21.
5. Ibid., November 16, 1954, p. 16.
6. Ibid., p. 17.
7. Ibid.
8. Ibid., November 19, 1954, p.1.
9. Freeman and Naftalin had worked together from 1944 to 1946 as aides to Humphrey in the mayor's office in Minneapolis. Naftalin joined the University of Minnesota faculty in 1946, leaving in 1948 to work in Washington, D.C., then returning to teach at the university in 1954. He worked as a volunteer in Humphrey's reelection campaign, in which the senator maintained offices apart from the DFL campaign headquarters that was political home to all the other candidates for state office. The distance was more than geographic, with personal suspicions inevitably triggering staff mistrust and jealousy. Only an individual in whom the governor had absolute political trust could occupy the highly sensitive post of the commissioner of administration. Freeman discussed the need with Dorothy Jacobson, campaign aide and trusted advisor. After Freeman described his frustration in finding a candidate, Jacobson, sensitive to the tensions of staff rivalries, urged him to consider Naftalin. While Freeman would manage his relationship with Humphrey personally, those relations might be compromised by portrayal of

his "deputy governor" as Senator Humphrey's man in state government. Freeman resolved the issue in a personal meeting with Naftalin. Responding to Freeman's questions, Naftalin declared that as a commissioner he would work for the governor. By clearing the air early, the men developed a close working relationship that grew into deep fondness and mutual professional admiration. After his stint in state government, Naftalin returned to the university; later he served three terms as Minneapolis mayor.

10. *Minneapolis Tribune,* November 24, 1954, p. 1.

11. On the advice of Freeman, President John F. Kennedy in 1961 appointed Heller the head of the Council of Economic Advisors. Heller advised Kennedy to raise taxes early in the new administration, an action recognized subsequently as the key step in providing the economic stability that unlocked the growth in the U.S. economy that followed. At the end of his service as the president's chief economic counselor, Heller returned in 1964 to become dean of the University of Minnesota School of Economics.

12. *Minneapolis Tribune,* November 26, 1955, p. 27.

13. Jacobson also was responsible for liaison with press and reporters, though she detested both. As a result, Tom Hughes managed press relations during Freeman's first term. Jacobson accompanied Freeman to Washington, D.C., as an advisor on international policy when in 1960 he became secretary of agriculture in the Kennedy administration. Subsequently Jacobson was the first woman appointed an assistant secretary of agriculture and the first to hold a presidential appointment (by President Lyndon B. Johnson) in the department. The opportunity arose when Johnson called Freeman to insist that more women be appointed to subcabinet posts in all departments. Freeman immediately sent Jacobson's name to the White House; the rest is history.

14. Robertson had been a tank commander serving in the European theater in World War II. A Kentuckian, he earned a master's degree in economics at the University of Minnesota, where he first met Walter Heller.

15. Hursh was president of the Wisconsin Welfare Council. In the 1930s, he worked in the Minnesota Governor's Office as secretary to Governors Olson, Benson, and Hjalmer Peterson.

16. Selke was a generation older than the new DFL leaders gathering around Freeman. An administrator of the Marshall Plan in Europe after World War II, he had returned to Minnesota, served as president of St. Cloud Teachers College (later St. Cloud State University), and retired.

17. Political analysts look back to the arrival of the DFL in 1954 as a preview of the political upheaval then building in the midwestern states. Four years later, in 1958, Democratic governors served in all states, except South Dakota, contingent with Minnesota.

18. The iron-ore industry of Minnesota's Iron Range paid an extraction tonnage fee to be set aside in a trust fund. The revenues from investment earnings are dedicated to economic-development programs in the region. In 1955 the

trust fund became the second largest in the nation, zealously guarded by Iron Range legislators.

19. If Freeman brought the DFL into postwar confrontation with the social, economic, and political realities of the second half of the 20th century, no less a battle occurred with Minnesota Senate Conservatives over state tax policy. See chapter 6: "The Battle over Withholding."

20. The *Minneapolis Sunday Tribune,* November 30, 1955, in a page-one analysis of the approaching 1956 legislative session, noted: "Freeman's election dooms the sales tax in 1955." It further suggested that "his pledge to support an increase in state per pupil basic aid from $80 to $92" had aggravated the tax situation.

21. *Governor's Weekly Report,* April 1954.

22. Minnesota editors, however, remained wrankled by Freeman's opposition to a sales tax. Donald J. Olson, editor of the *Marshall Messenger,* was perturbed: "Postponing a sales tax amounts simply to delaying the inevitable." Jack Scudder, editor of the *Little Falls Transcript,* agreed: "The sales tax is necessary, whether we like it or not." Edward J. Morrison, editor of the *Morris Sun,* argued for beer drinkers and cigarette smokers that "a general sales tax should replace all special sales taxes."

23. Mondale, a close personal friend of Tom Hughes, who was by this time Freeman's executive secretary, had been drafted along with Hughes in 1952 into the U.S. Army during the Korean War.

24. Stevenson's studied disinterest was less a desire to get out of the way of the Eisenhower campaign than a need to soothe bruises resulting from DFL Party squabbles during the presidential primaries. Humphrey, Freeman, and many DFL leaders had endorsed Stevenson, while a DFL faction that included Coya Knutson, the only woman in Minnesota's congressional delegation, rejected Stevenson in favor of Estes Kefauver of Tennessee. Kefauver had gained national attention as chair of a U.S. Senate committee investigating racketeering. At first reluctant to oppose Humphrey, Kefauver entered the Minnesota primary, defeating Stevenson and denying Humphrey and Freeman leadership of the Minnesota delegation to the 1956 Democratic convention. Humphrey served as chair of the Stevenson campaign in Minnesota, but Stevenson's campaign staff understandably was upset that Freeman and the DFL made what seemed only a token effort for the national party.

25. Arthur Naftalin interview by author, June 1999.

26. The Minnesota Legislature recovered its political balance in the 1957 session. Naftalin continued to chair the committee recommending state capital spending but forgo the power to decide ties when the votes split.

27. Campaign document, OLF Papers, MHS.

28. OLF Papers, MHS.

29. Ibid. On several occasions the tape for a radio program failed timely delivery to the broadcasting station. In such case, the station played music, announc-

ing that "the following program is presented for your enjoyment by the Freeman for Governor Committee." Some members of the campaign staff thought these incidents worked to the candidate's advantage, an idea not always shared by the candidate when he tuned in.

30. Ibid.
31. Ibid.
32. *Minneapolis Tribune,* September 27, 1956, p. 17.
33. Ibid., September 28, 1956, p. 21.
34. Ibid., September 30, 1956, p. 1.
35. Ibid., October 2, 1956, p. 1.
36. Ibid., October 5, 1956.
37. Ibid.
38. Ibid., October 6, 1956, p. 34.
39. Ibid., October 9, 1956, p. 3.
40. Ibid., October 11, 1956, p. 17.
41. Ibid., October 13, 1956, p. 7.
42. Ibid., October 27, 1956, p. 27.
43. Ibid., October 28, 1956, p.1.
44. Ibid., November 4, 1956, p.1.
45. Ibid.
46. Ibid., November 1, 1956, p. 1.
47. Ibid., November 7, 1956, p. 1.
48. Ibid., November 14, 1956, p. 14.
49. Ibid., November 18, 1956, p. 19A.
50. Ibid., November 23, 1956, p. 2.

Chapter 4

1. *Minneapolis Star,* January 14, 1957.
2. *Minneapolis Tribune,* April 12, 1957.
3. Ibid., April 13, 1957. Lilly referred to a suggestion that Minnesota might need new sources of tax revenue, including a sales tax, in the future. In 1957 no new sources of tax revenue were needed or proposed.
4. Fraser was one of 17 Liberals against a 50-member Conservative majority. By comparison, 69 Liberals—that is, the DFL—formed the majority caucus in the Minnesota House over 62 Conservatives.
5. Ibid.
6. *Minneapolis Tribune,* April 16, 1957, editorial page.
7. Ibid., April 27, 1957. Two of the three commissioners at the time were DFL members; neither supported the reorganization proposal.
8. *Minneapolis Tribune,* May 5, 1957.
9. Ibid.
10. Ibid., May 9, 1957. Freeman contemplated a line-item veto of a $1.1 million appropriation for the celebration of Minnesota's Centennial in 1958. He

asked for $500,000—more than adequate, he felt. He chose not to make an issue of the matter as the DFL House leadership had pushed for the higher amount. When the Centennial wound down, some $500,000 remained unspent. Freeman proposed returning the surplus to the state treasury, but the Centennial Commission voted to give it to public television for a new studio.

11. Freeman described Humphrey as "being all over the place."

12. A subsequent discussion with Sen. Ed Muskie on the floor of the U.S. Senate in 1959 confirmed for Freeman that he had made the right choice. Muskie, governor of Maine before being elected to the Senate, told Freeman he was happiest as governor, where he could make decisions and be responsible for managing state government. He said he never felt comfortable in the Senate.

13. OLF in a personal comment to the author, October 1998.

14. Gerald Heaney interview by author, August 1999.

15. *Minneapolis Tribune,* April 13, p. 1.

16. *Minneapolis Star,* May 24, 1958, p 11. Heaney and Clinton Boo, McCarthy's administrative assistant, told Wallace Mitchell, the *Star's* veteran political reporter, that they had nailed down the McCarthy victory 24 hours before the balloting. Mitchell wrote that McCarthy's strength was in the Twin Cities and the Iron Range, while Anderson's support came from outside the populous counties. Without detailing the trade for an endorsement of Knutson, Mitchell explained that Ninth District officials had agreed to shift votes on the second ballot to give McCarthy the outstate support he needed.

17. *Minneapolis Tribune,* April 20, 1958, (Upper Midwest Section), p. 2. Coya Knutson, Seventh District Congresswoman, pledged to Ray Hemenway, state DFL chair, that she would support the DFL Senate nominee endorsed at the state convention. Knutson, together with for Gov. Hjalmer Peterson and DFL maverick Robert Short, had led Estes Kefauver's primary challenge of Adlai Stevenson in 1956. Knutson needed help in getting endorsement for re-election in 1958, and Short had been rejected in Hennepin County as a delegate to the state DFL convention.

18. Arvonne Fraser interview by author, September 1999.

19. Two years later when Attorney General Miles Lord resigned as campaign planning began early in 1960, Freeman appointed Mondale attorney general of Minnesota, launching his political career. The decision carried risks to his own campaign, Freeman worried, but he believed Mondale the best choice.

20. OLF to Gov. Foster Furcolo of Massachusetts, August 20, 1958, OLF Papers.

21. The Freeman campaign spent $135,696 in the 1958 election. "Volunteer committees" for other DFL candidates collected more than $4,400, including $500 for McCarthy. DFL county headquarter committees and registration drives collected another $4,400.

22. *Overall Campaign Techniques* (1958), OLF Papers, MHS.

23. Mondale was adroit in managing volunteers, especially in outstate swings through congressional districts. After a decade of campaigning, however, he

opted for a cadre of paid professionals at the campaign center who he could hold to a higher performance level than a volunteer staff, no matter how committed.

24. Minnesota's GOP endorsed Nelsen for Congress in the Second District. He went on to win the election and return to Congress.
25. *Minneapolis Tribune,* April 17, 1958, p. 17.
26. Ibid.
27. Ibid., April 19, 1958, Upper Midwest Section, p. 1.
28. *Minneapolis Sunday Tribune,* June 8, 1958, p. 1.
29. Ibid., April 20, p. 1B.
30. *Minneapolis Tribune,* April 23, 1958, p. 1.
31. Jacobson, a key policy advisor, was Freeman's chief speechwriter, his social conscience in the Governor's Office, and a DFL activist intent on building a strong party.
32. Dorothy Jacobson Papers, MHS.
33. The *Minneapolis Star* endorsed Freeman October 28, 1958.
34. *Minneapolis Tribune,* April 19, 1958, p. 28. Solomon Barker, economist for the American Textile Workers union, predicted the 1958 recession would end in three months but that joblessness would persist.
35. The Minnesota Legislature met biennially (every two years), which meant that revenue estimates and funding appropriations had to cover a 24-month period. Anticipating revenues to be collected three years hence was a particularly speculative endeavor in the midst of the 1958 recession.
36. One irony of the 1958 campaign was that in electing a Catholic senator, the DFL would strengthen the prospects of John F. Kennedy winning the Democratic nomination for president in 1960 over Sen. Hubert H. Humphrey. Fletcher Knebel wrote in the *Minneapolis Star* on November 9, 1958, that, with Catholic successes in the 1958 elections, "the nomination of a Catholic in 1960 becomes a distinct possibility. If a Catholic can win in Minnesota, he can run anywhere."
37. Whenever his staff and advisors persisted in their attempts to get Freeman to change his mind, his ultimate response—preceding acceptance of their advice—was, "You're trying to make a political eunuch out of me."
38. The *Star* wanted Freeman to discuss state finances "in more detail," but the paper ran no report on the tax speech other than mentioning it in a political roundup column (October 30, Section B, p. 13) pertaining mainly to the Senate contest between GOP Sen. Ed Thye and DFL Rep. Gene McCarthy.
39. *Minneapolis Star,* October 30, 1958.

Chapter 5

1. Key state officials were widely scattered. Sieben was in Albert Lea, Freeman in Kandiyohi (city), Hughes in St. Paul, the attorney general at his home, and Maj. Gen. Joseph E. Nelson, commander of the Minnesota National Guard,

at home as well. Anticipating the need for quick decisions and action, Freeman had designated Tom Hughes the central coordinator.

2. *Minneapolis Tribune,* December 12, 1959, p.1.

3. Freeman repeated his conversation with General Nelson so many times that the recitation resembled a feedback loop. This version is based on an amalgamation of articles and personal reminiscences from over the past 40 years.

4. Ibid.

5. Ibid.

6. Cheri Register, *Packinghouse Daughter* (St. Paul: MHS Press, 2000), 198.

7. Winifred G. Helmes, *John A. Johnson: The People's Governor* (Minneapolis: University of Minnesota Press, 1949).

8. The Western Federation of Miners (WFM) in 1905 was a member of the American Federation of Labor (AFL), a trade union in which industrial workers found an uneasy fit. The WFM left the AFL in 1905 to join the Industrial Workers of the World (IWW or "Wobblies"). Unhappy in the IWW, the WFM seceded in 1907. It rejoined the AFL in 1912.

9. The primary source for material on the Teamster strike on 1934 in Minneapolis is Phillip A. Korth, *The Minneapolis Teamster Strike of 1934* (East Lansing: Michigan State University Press, 1995).

10. *Minneapolis Star,* August 7, 1934, p.1.

11. *Minneapolis Star,* August 12, 1934, p.1.

12. *Minneapolis Tribune,* December 9, 1958, p.1.

13. Ibid., December 13, 1959, p. 1.

14. Ibid., December 29, 1959, p.1.

15. Courts have the implied constitutional authority to determine when statutes or rules (actions by legislative or executive bodies) violate the constitutions of states or of the federal government. Courts, however, have no authority to rule on or to amend constitutional provisions.

Chapter 6

1. Outgoing Gov. C. Elmer Anderson offered to appoint Naftalin commissioner of administration to ease transition for the new administration. Freeman gratefully accepted.

2. A pay-as-you-go tax system inaugurated on July 1, 1955, would collect three years of income taxes in two years. In 1955 state taxpayers were to pay one-half of the 1955 tax and the entire 1954 tax obligation. In 1956 they would pay all of the tax obligation for that year plus the remaining half of the 1955 obligation.

3. The deficit was $40 million, but Freeman asked for a $50 million increase so as to designate $10 million for a rainy-day fund.

4. The lower level of per-pupil assistance reduced the deficit to about $30 million. Sooner-than-expected increases in income taxes raised revenues $6 million beyond those estimated, leaving a manageable deficit of $24 million.

5. *1956 Report of the Governor's Minnesota Tax Study Committee* (J. Cameron Thomson Study), December 27, 1956.
6. *Minneapolis Sunday Tribune,* December 30, 1956, p. 5B.
7. Ibid.
8. The *Minneapolis Sunday Tribune* applauded the committee's report, released on December 27, 1956, as "evidence to business and industry leaders of the nation that Minnesota is seriously interested in improving the climate for business and industry expansion." The editorialist noted that "national publications had sent staff to cover the press conference announcing the unanimous report [proposing] a more equitable tax system to provide new incentives for economic growth and at the same time provide necessary funds for state and local government." The *Tribune* called the report "a realistic appraisal of Minnesota's economic outlook and the tax encouragement that must be given to assure economic growth. The committee members and chairman J. Cameron Thomson deserve our thanks." The editorial on the Governor's Tax Study Committee did not mention Freeman by name.
9. OLF Papers, MHS.
10. The legislature adopted Freeman's government reorganization proposal in 1955, but the Minnesota Supreme Court threw out the statute on a technical error. The clerk of the House had failed to follow the rules for engrossing, or entering the bill in the statutory records.
11. *Minneapolis Tribune,* January 15, 1959, p. 1.
12. Ibid., January 14, 1959.
13. The legislature actually appropriated $487.7 million, compared with the $488.5 requested by Freeman, a difference of about $790,000 or less than 0.02 percent.
14. Ibid.
15. One-half of state senators originally were to be elected every two years for four-year terms. When the legislature adopted Minnesota's constitution in 1858, however, it adopted two competing versions, one with half the Senate elected every two years and the other with four-year terms. It never resolved the conflict, but the four-year tradition took hold and remains in practice.
16. Karl Grittner, Oral Histories, 1970, Minnesota Government, MHS. Grittner represented the new political vigor brought to Minnesota politics by Freeman and the DFL. As a state senator, he embodied the philosophy of Minnesota liberalism in the relationship between government and the citizen. "Taxes are something you don't talk about, but almost all the income we have in state government is the result of a tax program. Government, if it wishes to provide more services, has to get more money. There's only one way to do it and that's to increase taxes," he said.
17. *Minneapolis Tribune,* April 22, 1959, p. 1.
18. When Harold Schultz, a DFLer from St. Paul, asked for a progress report on the conference committee, the *Minneapolis Star* (April 24) reported that

Wright said, "It's a little late for that." Schultz replied, "That's not the answer I expected."

19. *Minneapolis Tribune,* April 25, 1959, p. 1.
20. *Minneapolis Tribune,* May 5, 1959.
21. Ibid., May 6, 1959.
22. *Minneapolis Star,* June 19, 1959, p. 7.
23. Joe Robertson, Minnesota tax commissioner, in a May 26 memo to Freeman on alternative tax plans, said Wright "seems to have a *genuine* conviction that withheld taxes *are* built into wage rates while sales taxes aren't—on which, I think, he's dead wrong." Nothing, not even the fact that federal pay-as-you-go did not cause wage increases, could dissuade Wright. The Minnesota Legislature traditionally practices a sense of comity and civility between House and Senate. The 1959 legislature demonstrated that comity is a reflection of the political consensus in the state, and both were shattered. Minnesota liberalism was emerging as the dominant political philosophy. For Conservative senators, the concept of withholding, a method for collecting taxes, embodied that liberal philosophy.
24. The Eisenhower farm program took a political toll on Republicans. Membership in the Minnesota Farmers Union had increased significantly during the 1950s as farmers shifted away from the conservative Minnesota Farm Bureau, building the Farmers Union membership into the largest farm group in Minnesota.
25. OLF Papers, MHS.
26. The Minnesota Poll, *Minneapolis Tribune,* July 5, 1959, found in June that public support for withholding was 64 percent, a seven-point increase over year-earlier levels.
27. "Joe Robertson has suggested, wisely I think, that there be no identification of names, though anybody who works at it could figure out from whom and to whom it's directed!" Heller wrote in a covering memo. OLF Papers, MHS.
28. OLF Papers, MHS.
29. Ibid.
30. Gerald Heaney to OLF, June 10, 1959. OLF Papers, MHS.
31. *Minneapolis Tribune,* June 22, 1959
32. Ibid., June 24, 1959.
33. Memorandum from Arthur Naftalin, Commissioner of Administration, June 20, 1959, OLF Papers, MHS.
34. *Minneapolis Tribune,* June 30, 1959.
35. Ibid., June 30, 1959.
36. Ibid., July 2, 1959.
37. Ibid., June 26, 1959; *Minneapolis Star,* June 25, 1959.
38. Dorothy Jacobson, Freeman's assistant for policy, drafted the statement. See "1955–60 miscellaneous folder," File of Staff Assistant Rodney Leonard, Governor Freeman Records, OLF Papers, MHS.

Chapter 7

1. Commissioner of Administration Arthur Naftalin (1954–1960) described a meeting in the governor's office in which he asked Freeman for directions on six issues. Naftalin began by identifying the issues in an informal agenda. Halfway through the discussion, believing too little time was available, Naftalin passed over three items, skipping to the sixth. After resolving the third of the priority issues, Naftalin thanked Freeman and rose to leave. Freeman enumerated the three remaining issues and, as Naftalin presented the options, quickly disposed of each. As commissioner, Naftalin acted as a deputy governor, directing the day-by-day workings of agencies reporting to the Office of the Governor. Freeman trusted Naftalin to bring in matters of importance, intuitively aware that making no decision was a decision to transfer authority elsewhere. Arthur Naftalin interview by author, Minneapolis, November 2002.

2. OLF interivew by Hyman Berman and Carl Ross, August 5, 1988, 20th Century Radicalism in Minnesota, Oral History, MHS.

3. Humphrey once urged Freeman to understand that the role of a candidate is different from that of a governor: "[We] get so accustomed to fighting and being a candidate with an uphill battle that when one does become an officeholder, it is kind of difficult to adjust to the new situation." Humphrey to OLF, May 17, 1956, OLF Papers, MHS.

4. The functional organization of the Office of Governor, although never formally defined, illustrates the intuitive managerial skill in decision making that Freeman brought and continually refined during his tenure. Thomas Hughes, executive assistant to the governor and former secretary of the DFL Party, continued as political liaison with the chair of the DFL, Ray Hemenway, other district and county political leaders, and DFL legislators. Hemenway, often inarticulate and rough-spoken, became party disciplinarian with no trouble being understood. Dorothy Jacobson, a member of the DFL executive committee and associate professor of political science at Macalester College, became the information center of the governor's office, digesting and melding a prodigious flow of public-policy issues with an endless stream of data from state agencies on social, economic, and educational programs into policy memorandum, messages, speeches, and analyses. Arthur Naftalin, Commissioner of Administration, could visualize and describe a coherence in the working pattern of agency relationships that seemed chaotic to everyone around him. Walter Heller, although never appearing on an organization chart, brought remarkably sophisticated insight to tax and financial policy from his position as a professor of economics at the University of Minnesota.

5. OLF interview by Hyman Berman and Carl Ross, August 5, 1988, 20th Century Radicalism in Minnesota, Oral History, MHS.

6. Applying the same ratio to tax implications of Minnesota's current budget deficits, Freeman's budget proposals for the 1955–56 biennium to raise

about $20 million of a $50 million deficit from higher corporate tax obligations would equate to a $1.8 billion increase in corporate tax obligation in
2004–05.

7. In the first year of withholding, wage earners would pay taxes March (now
April) 15 on wages earned in the previous year. Withholding would begin
July 1, the start of Minnesota's fiscal year, which meant they would pay the
equivalent of 1.5 years in income taxes in the first year. In the second year of
withholding, they would owe a lump-sum tax payment on March 15 for the
six months wages were not withheld in the first year of withholding. Their
wages would be withheld for the full year, to pay the equivalent of 1.5 years
in income taxes the second year.

8. Arthur Naftalin interview by author, May 1999.

9. Chapter 6: "The Battle over Withholding" includes a more detailed discussion of the Minnesota Tax Study Committee.

10. OLF Papers, MHS.

11. Ibid.

12. The epilogue examines the 1960s legislative battles over tax policy.

13. When the Department of Highways told Governor Freeman that historic
Fort Snelling above the Mississippi River had to be destroyed for a four-lane
highway and traffic exchange to ensure access to the new Twin Cities airport,
he suggested a tunnel under the fort. Fort Snelling would remain undistubed,
the engineers would get their highway, and travelers would have easy airport
access. The discussion ended.

14. The dictionary defines *compassion* as a feeling of pity, a definition that is in
conflict with the meaning and use of the term by Christian scholars who view
compassion as a sense of empathy, an expression of civic virtue, and a basis
for a social system oriented toward community. Compassion differs from pity
and mercy, terms that imply a relationship between a superior and an inferior, a situation in which one is more holy than the other. See Marcus J.
Borg, *Meeting Jesus Again for the First Time* (San Francisco: Harper, 1995).

15. The epilogue discusses the governors of the 1960s in more detail.

Chapter 8

1. An early-morning phone call on December 12, 1960, from President-elect
John F. Kennedy galvanized Governor Freeman, lifting the pall of gloom that
had settled over the Freeman household following his 50.4 to 49.6 percent
loss in November to Elmer L. Andersen. Kennedy asked Freeman to join his
cabinet as secretary of agriculture in 1961. If Freeman accepted, the president-elect said, Freeman should be in Washington, D.C., that afternoon for a
press-conference announcement of the appointment. Freeman accepted,
thanking the president-elect. In the last exercise of his prerogatives as governor, Freeman ordered a National Guard jet readied to fly him into a new
chapter of his life. He reached the nation's capital with time to spare.

2. Minnesota senators serve four-year terms while House members serve two years. The Senate had last been elected in 1958, and many members faced campaigning in new districts realigned by the 1960 census. Facing new voters was another reason to avoid the sales tax.

3. *Minneapolis Tribune,* April 12, 1961, p. 1. The withholding proposal was essentially the same as the one Freeman had been willing to accept in the 1959 special session; Senate Conservatives had rejected it. The technical argument for early enactment was good management. The Minnesota Tax Department needed time to complete the paperwork related to implementing withholding to meet the July 1 deadline (the 1961 fiscal year began then).

4. *Minneapolis Tribune,* April 22, 1961, p.1.

5. Ibid., April 26, 1961, p.1.

6. Ibid.

7. Ibid., May 3, 1961, p.1.

8. Ibid.

9. Ibid., May 30, 1961, p.1.

10. The election was historic for several reasons. The winner would be the first Minnesota governor to serve a four-year term.

11. Rolvaag's erratic behavior did not play well with Minnesota voters. In May 1965 the Minnesota Poll found only 39 percent of voters viewed him approvingly.

12. The *Minneapolis Tribune,* May 27, 1957 (editorial page), subsequently dismissed LeVander's promise to veto any sales-tax bill as an "ill-advised campaign pledge."

13. Minnesota budget message, February 14, 1967. See *Minneapolis Tribune,* February 5, 1967, p.1.

14. The Conservative designation may have led some voters to believe Conservatives were different from Republicans, underscoring the virtue of Freemen's belief that political parties must be held accountable for public policies. If the difference confused voters, the political cover was modest. Only two political parties vied for control of the Minnesota Legislature. The DFL wore its party label openly. The Republican Party chose the Conservative label.

15. *Minneapolis Tribune,* April 28, 1967, p. 1.

16. Ibid., April 30, 1967, p. 1.

17. Graven, a rising star in DFL politics, quickly faded from prominence after the sales-tax campaign. While his stance on taxes did not endear him to the DFL, his political luster was tarnished primarily when his wife won a divorce charging physical abuse.

18. *Minneapolis Tribune,* May 1, 1967, p. 1.

19. Ibid., May 6, 1967, p. 1. The editors and the publisher of the *Tribune* determine the topics for polling and the timing of their publication. A decade earlier, when Governor Freeman was locked in the longest (to date) special session in Minnesota history over tax policy regarding the withholding of state

income taxes from wage-earners, the *Tribune* published polling data that found more than 60 percent of voters supported withholding only after the special session ended. Freeman had proposed withholding in lieu of higher taxes, but the plan was not adopted.

20. Ibid., May 17, 1967, p.1.
21. Ibid., May 18, 1967, p.1. An excise tax is a sales tax, usually applied to specific products or services, such as gasoline or cigarettes. Governor LeVander said that Senator Wright's excise tax was a general sales tax.
22. Ibid., May 20, 1967, p. 1.
23. Ibid. The regular session of the 1967 legislature officially ended at midnight on May 20, leaving the legislature one day to override Governor LeVander's veto. If he had held the bill for 24 hours—that is, put the bill in his pocket, using a "pocket" veto—the tax proposal would have died.
24. Ibid., May 21, 1967, p. 1.
25. Ibid., May 24, 1967, p. 1.
26. The *Minneapolis Tribune,* May 25, 1967, editorially chastised LeVander, calling his tax-relief package "a halfway measure." The editors blamed this result on an "ill-advised late campaign speech opposing a sales tax." The editorialist earlier had pleaded with the Minnesota DFL to be more like Iowa Democrats. They supported a sales tax, he opined, so why not the DFL?
27. Ibid., May 27, 1967, p. 1.
28. Ibid., May 28, 1967, p. 1.
29. Ibid., May 30, 1967, p. 1.
30. Ibid., June 2, 1967, p. 1.
31. Ibid., April 16, 1969, p.1.
32. Ibid.
33. Ibid.
34. *Minneapolis Star,* January 5, 1971, p. 1.
35. Ibid., January 24, 1971, p.1.
36. Ibid., January 27, 1971, p. 1.
37. *Minneapolis Tribune,* January 2, 1971, p. 12A.
38. *Minneapolis Star,* January 27, 1971, p. 1.
39. Ibid., July 2, 1871, p. 1.
40. Ibid., August 4, 1971, p. 1.
41. Ibid., September 7, 1971, p. 1.
42. Ibid., October 15, 1971, p.1.
43. Only a third of the Senate Conservatives and some four of every ten House Conservatives voted for the tax bill. *Minneapolis Tribune,* October 31, 1971, p. 1.

Sources

The Minnesota Historical Society is the main repository of information about Gov. Orville L. Freeman (OLF). Resources there include:

The OLF Papers
   Campaign documents
   Correspondence and reports to and/or from:
      OLF
      Gerald Heaney
      Hubert H. Humphrey
      Duluth union officials
      John Bystrom
      Mitch Perrazo
      Foster Furcolo (governor of Massachusetts)
      Arthur Naftalin
      Rodney Leonard
   Governor's Weekly Report, April 1954.
   Overall Campaign Techniques, 1958.

DFL Central Committee Files
Dorothy Jacobson Papers
Oral History
   Minnesota Government: Karl Grittner, 1970.
   20th Century Radicalism in Minnesota: OLF interview by Hyman Berman and Carl Ross, August 5, 1988.

Newspapers (available on microfilm)
Little Falls Transcript
Marshall Messenger
Minneapolis Star
Minneapolis Tribune
Morris Sun
St. Paul Dispatch
St. Paul Pioneer Press

Other resources include:

Articles
Cato, Robert. "The Orator of the Dawn," *The New Yorker* (March 4, 2002): 46–63.

Books
Borg, Marcus J. *Meeting Jesus Again for the First Time.* San Francisco: Harper, 1995.

Carnes, Mark C., and John A. Garraty, with Patrick Williams. *Mapping America's Past: A Historical Atlas.* New York: Henry Holt, 1966.

Helmes, Winifred G. *John A. Johnson: The People's Governor.* Minneapolis: University of Minnesota Press, 1949.

Korth, Phillip A. *The Minneapolis Teamster Strike of 1934.* East Lansing: Michigan State University Press, 1995.

1956 Report of the Governor's Minnesota Tax Study Committee. J. Cameron Thomson Study, December 27, 1956.

Register, Cheri. *Packinghouse Daughter.* St. Paul: MHS Press, 2000.

Interviews by the Author
Arvonne Fraser, May and September 1999.
Orville L. Freeman, October 1998.
Gerald Heaney, June and August 1999.
Bill Kubicek, August 1999.
Arthur Naftalin, June 1999 and November 2002.

Index

Photos are indicated by numbers in italic at the ends of entries.

Orville L. Freeman and Rod Leonard

About the Author

Rod Leonard lives on an 80-acre farm near Wahkon, Minnesota, a stone's throw from Lake Mille Lacs. There he is "caretaker" for deer, eagles, crows, owls, coyotes, wolves, bears, possums, badgers, porcupine, squirrels, and chipmunks. Other wildlife includes an occasional grandchild.

Leonard met Elizabeth (Betty) Berg at the University of Minnesota; both were senior editors of the *Minnesota Daily*. They married in 1955 and over the next decade had three children—twins, Jane and Karin, and a son, John. In 1957 Rod joined Governor Freeman's staff as press secretary. In 1961 he joined Freeman, named President John F. Kennedy's Secretary of Agriculture, in Washington, D.C. In 1969 Leonard founded the Community Nutrition Institute, which he still heads, and in 1978–79 he served in the Carter White House as deputy director of the U.S. Office of Consumer Affairs. The Leonards retired to Betty's family farm in 1998; Betty died in 2001.